Wallcovering Secrets

from Brian Santos
The Wall Wizard

Meredith® Books
Des Moines, Iowa

Wallcovering Secrets from the Wall Wizard
Editor: Larry Johnston
Contributing Writer: Dan Weeks
Copy Chief: Terri Fredrickson
Copy Editor: Kevin Cox
Publishing Operations Manager: Karen Schirm
Senior Editor, Asset & Information Management: Phillip Morgan
Edit and Design Production Coordinator: Mary Lee Gavin
Editorial and Design Assistant: Renee E. McAtee
Book Production Managers: Pam Kvitne, Marjorie J. Schenkelberg,
　Rick von Holdt, Mark Weaver
Imaging Center Operator: Maggie M. Gulling
Contributing Copy Editor: Andrea Kline
Contributing Proofreaders: Sara Henderson, Heidi Johnson, Cheri Madison
Contributing Indexer: Don Glassman
Other Contributors: Janet Anderson

**Additional Editorial Contributions from
　Abramowitz Creative Studios**
Publishing Director/Designer: Tim Abramowitz
Illustrator/Designer: Kelly Bailey
Designer: Joel Wires

Hetherington Studios
Director of Photography: Douglas Hetherington
Operations Manager/Model: Mara Hetherington
Production: Doug Rieck

Meredith® Books
Editor in Chief: Gregory H. Kayko
Executive Director, Design: Matt Strelecki
Managing Editor: Amy Tincher-Durik
Executive Editor/Group Manager: Benjamin W. Allen
Associate Design Director: Chad Jewell
Marketing Product Manager: Brent Wiersma

Executive Director, Marketing: Kevin Kacere
Editorial Director: Linda Raglan Cunningham
Executive Director, New Business Development: Todd M. Davis
Executive Director, Sales: Ken Zagor
Director, Operations: George A. Susral
Director, Production: Douglas M. Johnston
Director, Marketing & Publicity: Amy Nichols
Business Director: Jim Leonard

Vice President and General Manager: Douglas J. Guendel

Meredith Publishing Group
President: Jack Griffin
Senior Vice President: Karla Jeffries

Meredith Corporation
Chairman of the Board: William T. Kerr
President and Chief Executive Officer: Stephen M. Lacy

In Memoriam: E.T. Meredith III (1933–2003)

Thanks to
Blue Mountain Wallcoverings, Inc.

Library of Congress Control Number: 2007921717
ISBN: 978-0-696-23475-0

All of us at Meredith® Books are dedicated to providing
you with the information and ideas you need to enhance
your home and garden. We welcome your comments and
suggestions. Write to us at:
Meredith Books
Home Improvement Books Department
1716 Locust St.
Des Moines, IA 50309–3023

Note to the Readers: Due to differing conditions, tools,
and individual skills, Meredith Corporation assumes no
responsibility for any damages, injuries suffered, or losses
incurred as a result of following the information published
in this book. Before beginning any project, review the
instructions carefully, and if any doubts or questions
remain, consult local experts or authorities. Because codes
and regulations vary greatly, you always should check
with authorities to ensure that your project complies
with all applicable local codes and regulations. Always
read and observe all of the safety precautions provided by
manufacturers of any tools, equipment, or supplies, and
follow all accepted safety procedures.

Dedication

This book is dedicated to the future.

To understand the future you have to look to the past. Wallcoverings have been a part of interior design for a millennium—from the most primitive wallhangings to tapestries, handprinted papers, and now high-tech, modular coverings that expand the definition of wall treatments. These advances bring all the richness, history, and culture of the past into the future. That gives you the power to enrich your home's tone, mood, and look as never before.

Wallcoverings—whether used throughout your home or just as an accent border, wainscot, or feature wall—can add depth, design, and decorability in ways you could never imagine.

THANK-YOUS

It takes a village to raise a Wizard. My special thanks:

To my mom, for her artistic influence. To my dad, for his work ethic. To my grandfather, for instilling me with the power of *why*.

To Blue Mountain Wallcoverings, Inc., especially LeeAnne, John, Chris, Malcolm, and Dave for their creative vision, innovation, and brilliant execution. They're reinvigorating the wallcovering industry with their amazing efforts.

To Meredith Corporation and Larry, Dan, Doug, Chad, Tim, and Kelly for their belief in the magic of the Wizard.

To my children, Pal, Scott, and Kelli, whom I love and who are the future.

And most of all, to my wife and partner, Virginia, who shares all my dreams. Thank you for all your love and support throughout our journeys together.

Table of Contents

Chapter 1: Imagine the Possibilities

Chapter 2: Material Selection

Chapter 3: Preparation

Chapter 4: Application

Chapter 5: Finishing Touches

Meet the Wizard

"That's so cool! How do you do that?" I hear this all the time as I demonstrate how to apply wallcoverings in my workshops at home shows around the world. The question that inevitably follows my demonstration is "Can I do that?"

I always answer, "Yes, you can!" With an understanding of the materials and techniques involved, almost anyone can create beautiful rooms—especially now that new products make wallcoverings more user friendly and easier to work with than ever before. And once you know and master some basic principles, the variety of results you can create is virtually limitless.

I'm a fourth-generation wallcovering contractor. My philosophy is simple: *Knowledge is power.* The secret to success isn't in the tools, the materials, or the techniques—nor is it in the high-tech materials and adhesives that are available today. While impressive, these latest developments, which I explain thoroughly in this book, are only part of the formula for success.

The real secret to success lies in understanding how results are achieved. I call this the "why behind the how-to," and it is something most books, classes, and workshops never tell you. How can you know what to do if you don't understand why you're doing it? That's why I wrote this book: to reveal the science behind the magic and show you how to create some magic of your own.

First we'll look at some gorgeous rooms in several styles to see just how rich and varied your wallcovering options are. Then we'll talk about how to choose materials, what tools you'll need to do the job, and how to prepare the room—including my magic wallpaper stripping formula and method that allows you to strip up to 16 layers of wallcoverings at once. Then I'll share what I call the "Henry Ford method of installing wallcoverings." By following my sequential method, you'll apply wallcoverings faster, easier, and with less mess and frustration than many pros. Finally I'll tell you how you can master the challenges that frequently come up during application—and how to care for and maintain your wallcoverings so they look great for many years to come.

People say I'm an artist—a Wall Wizard—and I'm proud to agree. But the truth is, I learned how to create wallcovering effects by trial and error, experiment and failure. In more than 25 years of applying wallcoverings, I've made every kind of mistake you can think of—and lots more you can't even imagine. I pass on the lessons of those mistakes so you don't have to make them. I've come up with simple tips and tricks that'll make your project go smoothly and take much less time than conventional methods. They're all based on a combination of common sense and professional experience.

So let's get started!

Chapter 1

Imagine the Possibilities

Welcome to the magic of pattern and the power of texture! Nothing gives a room more aesthetic appeal with less effort and technical skill than wallcoverings. They can enhance your home's architecture and give your home a shot of color and design in any style and palette you can imagine. Wallcoverings should play an important part in your design choices.

Wallcoverings are also among the most affordable ways to effect a complete design transformation. A few bolts of wallcoverings cost considerably less than a new suite of furniture, bath fixtures, or kitchen appliances. Wallcoverings are the most practical, accessible—and overlooked—way of creating design and dimension in your home.

This book will show you how to transform your home through wallcoverings. A gallery of inspiring rooms in this chapter shows the tremendous range of styles and effects you can use to create drama and beauty anywhere in your house.

The rest of the book introduces you to the materials, tools, and techniques that will help you achieve decorating success. In my 25 years of teaching how to apply wallcoverings, it has become apparent that fear of the process keeps homeowners from taking advantage of the decorating power of wallcoverings. That's understandable: The techniques can seem daunting, especially if they have never been explained to you. But if you follow the steps in this book, you will be able to realize the joy that can come from creating an artful and expressive home interior.

Vintage Verve

Here's an eclectic Victorian style that's been orchestrated with exquisite taste. At least five different wallcoverings are used in this entryway, including a mitered frieze above the windows, a wrap-and-rope border that divides a lacy, lattice mosaic from a vertical stripe on the wall beneath the stairwell, and a Moorish-style border that runs around the top of the wall.

Quartersawn oak and parquet inlay—showcase materials not found in new construction—deserve a visual context that honors how special they are. That's just what the wallcoverings in this room do. In addition strong graphic elements in the wallcovering provide a pleasing offset to the organic quality of the wood. The result is stunning. But the best part is that the techniques required to execute such a treatment are not difficult—you'll learn them all in Chapter 4. What makes them all work so well together is an excellent choice of color, pattern, and scale. Wallcovering collections help you make those decorating decisions by packaging many complementary elements together so you don't have to be a professional interior designer to create a pleasing effect.

Pattern on Pattern

Everyone knows you shouldn't put stripes with plaids. So is it always bad to put different patterns together? Not always. As long as the graphic elements are in proportion and there's a common color theme, you can use complementary patterns to tell a story.

Each pattern is like a different chapter. In this hall the stripe adds height and the brocade adds texture. They work well together because few tones are used, maintaining a color continuity among graphic elements. The result is rich—even intricate—but harmonic.

Bold and Beautiful

This room illustrates the importance of balance, scale, and color. The repeat of the wallpaper pattern fits the scale of the furnishings perfectly, and the design is proportionate to the carved detail on the table. The diagonal rhythm of the pattern contrasts nicely with the formal, symmetric composition of this vignette. The wall inverts the color scheme of the table and plates—the cream-color background mimics the plates, and the green stems and leaves of the plants reflect the green table. It's a sophisticated effect but is extremely easy to achieve because the paper is a straight-across-match pattern that's one of the easiest types to apply.

The Pattern Paradox

The light, whimsical floral pattern offsets the formality and symmetry of this room's furniture and interior design. At the same time the pattern repeats with mathematical precision in a grid, reinforcing the room's formality and symmetry, giving the small space a presence it would otherwise lack.

A repeating pattern element—in this case the flower—and the scale and rhythm of the repetition individually affect the room's style and design. Together they bring about a look that neither the individual elements nor the pattern grid could produce on their own.

Organic Chemistry

With seven different patterns and only three colors, this room's design is not really focused on color; it's based on texture. The yellow (or its variant, caramel) and black create a vibrant, high-contrast pattern that defines the room. The wheat fleur-de-lis wallcovering pattern brings it all together, uniting the natural sisal carpet and wood furniture with the highly patterned window treatments. The wallcovering's rhythmic pattern and its curved, natural motif remain unobtrusive and allow the room's overall design and furnishings to shine. This room demonstrates that a bold effect doesn't always require a bold wallcovering pattern, simply the right mix of design elements. The tremendous variety of wallcovering patterns and colorways available gives you a broad visual vocabulary that lets you work magic like this.

Mix and Match

You can use more than one strong graphic element as long as you don't overdo the color scheme. Keep your choice of colors few and simple, and you'll find that even seemingly opposing design elements—structured vs. organic or crisp vs. soft—work well together.

Pattern Precision

In this room a repeating pattern creates a background for major decorating elements—beautiful pieces of handpainted furniture. The small-scale pattern makes the massive bed seem more intimate, and the white background with blue print complements the hue of the furniture while keeping the room visually light. Small-print patterns like this must be applied so the pattern matches precisely at the seams or the whole effect will be ruined. In this book you'll learn a fail-safe method of hanging every sheet of wallcovering straight and true and matching every seam with precision.

Comfort Zone

This visually rich space features plush period materials such as lace, velvet, and velour. Varied furniture scale—a heavy chair and a light table—helps make the room feel inviting. The design scheme layers tone on tone, pattern on pattern, and texture on texture for a sumptuous effect. The forest green wallcoverings with vertical stripe against a rich brocade show variety in texture and pattern more than color. The color provides a great backdrop to the landscape painting on the back wall. The wallcovering's textured effect implies padded, fabric-upholstered walls, but they're not—it's all done with off-the-roll wallcoverings and the techniques described in Chapter 4.

The Look and Feel

High-touch is good! You can achieve the effect relatively easily and inexpensively with wallcoverings. Today's wallcoverings are rich in color and texture; many simulate the look of expensive fabrics, leather, and other tactile materials. So don't be afraid to use textural elements to create a warm, cozy effect that can add to the serenity of your space.

Simulations

Even as a professional faux finisher, I'd be hard-pressed to create an effect as realistic as the brick- and stone-pattern wallcoverings on these two pages. Both demonstrate how a printing process combined with an embossed surface texture can create an illusion that's so convincing you'll have a hard time believing it came into the room in rolls. Few can have a hand-laid limestone or antique brick wall, but wallcoverings bring the visual effects of these surfaces within reach.

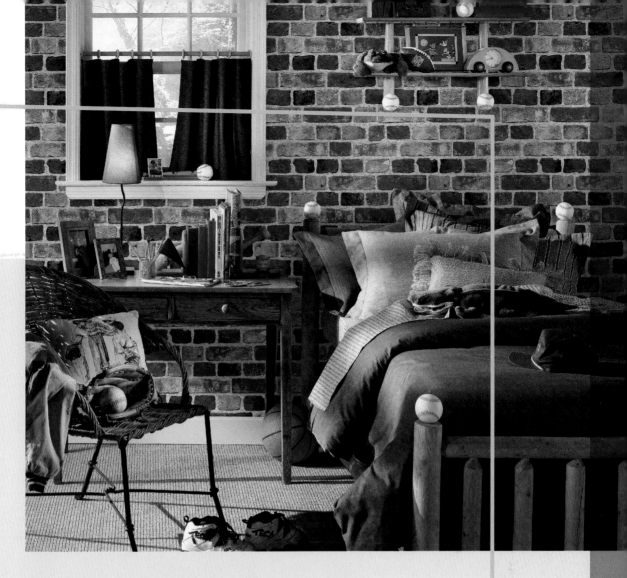

What You See Is
Not What You Get

Talk about illusion—check out these two rooms! What looks like weathered
brick and carefully fitted limestone are readily available wallcoverings. This is
an ideal way to add instant architectural character. In some cases wallcovering
manufacturers begin with photographs of the real stone or brick wall. The art
comes in convincingly rendering the image within the confines of a repeating
pattern. The two examples shown are drop match patterns in which the pattern
spreads across two sheets of wallcovering. This makes the pattern larger with
fewer repeats so the faux effect is even more convincing. There's no mystery
to hanging a drop match pattern, as you'll see on pages 118–119.

Know Your Own Mind

Base wallcovering selections on the style you want to achieve and don't be afraid to experiment. The color, rhythm, and strength of a pattern can change the weight and scale of a room dramatically. Only the wallcovering has changed in the four room settings shown on the opposite page, yet the look varies from bold to airy, the architecture from prominent to a mere background. So don't be afraid to try something imaginative—wallcoverings are not forever. You can always change your mind—and your decor—later.

One Room, Four Choices

By varying patterns, colors, and border heights, you can create completely different effects in the same space. Even though the fixtures and furnishings remain the same, these four baths have different styles and moods. And the cost of even the most expensive wallcoverings is far less than that of replacing all the furnishings and architectural features. Wallcovering, while more costly than paint, is less expensive than just about any other method to completely change the character of a room. To help you visualize ideas, wallcovering manufacturers are working on technology that will allow you to apply virtual wallcoverings to digital photos of your room so you can see the results before buying a single roll of material.

Depth of Field

Even with no art on the wall, minimalist furniture, and few accessories, this room appears deep, rich, and inviting, thanks to the wallcovering. The dark background makes the aluminum coffee table pop out and the minimalist microfiber couch appear to stand away from the wall, visually enlarging the room. The freeform design of the peonies and their bright color echo the color of the sofa fabric and lend texture, while the dark background provides a contrast that emphasizes the furniture's simple form. The three simple pieces of furniture gain stature from the richness of the background, demonstrating that wallcoverings can visually furnish a room with a minimum of clutter and expense.

The Background That Binds

A unifying background such as this peony-pattern wallcovering—with its range of colors, lines, and scales—can complement a varied collection of furnishings. If you have some favorite but disparate furnishings, accessories, or other elements you'd like to combine in a room, select a wallcovering that will help your eclectic possessions live happily together.

Accenting Architecture

This serene, modern Oriental-style room gains presence from a two-tone frottage-style wallcovering. The contrast between dark and light in the wallcovering adds visual depth and luster to the room, relieving the monochromatic scheme of the furnishings. Using the same wallcovering on two symmetrically placed folding screens increases the sense of depth and adds some architectural detail to an otherwise boring space. Find advice on applying wallcoverings to supporting elements in a room in Chapter 5.

Background Becomes Foreground

Moving wallcoverings off the wall and into the room—such as on the shoji screens here—gives a minimalist design richness and depth that it otherwise would not possess. This wallcovering also has a sheen that adds a shimmer that contrasts nicely to the matte finishes in the room.

Old Meets New

A bronze metallic foil printed with a suedelike pattern offers a contemporary rendering of a traditional brocade pattern. In this room the pattern's elaborate curvilinear design offsets the straight lines of the furnishings and adds movement. The fluid shapes and rhythmic pattern repeat lift the eye, and the suedelike nap changes subtly with light and point of view. Traditional patterns are often executed in the latest materials—such as this combination of metallic foil and synthetic, textured ink—because what's truly new has to resonate with the past to gain acceptance.

Foil wallcovering is cut, trimmed, and applied just like more traditional materials, but care is required to avoid creasing it and breaking the metallic sheen. Walls must be properly prepared for this or any high-gloss wallcovering because surface variations will telegraph through. The wall preparation steps in Chapter 3 show how to ready a wall for a top-quality job. A bonus: Metallic wallcoverings are washable.

The Gee Whiz Factor

To increase acceptance of wallcoverings, manufacturers want to make them easier to apply. Longstanding consumer objections to handling wallcoverings in long, rolled-up strips have brought one innovation, called ModulArt, which comes in $20\frac{1}{2}$-inch squares instead of rolls. The squares, made of a nonwoven material that's stable and prepasted, are shipped flat so there's no curling to deal with. Colors and textures can be mixed and matched to create a wide variety of effects. Squares of different colors can create a bold feature wall (below left) while cutting circles out of the squares creates a mod pattern (bottom right).

The material can easily be cut to any shape. Application steps are the same as for rolled materials, simplified by the easy-to-handle shape and size (see pages 164–165). To change decor the squares can be pulled off the wall—and even reused.

Chapter 2

Material Selection

You've seen how wallcoverings can change the look of a room. Now it's time to explore the material itself and decide which type of wallcovering—what scale, pattern, and color—will give the look you want. You have many choices—more than you probably can imagine—and your selections will affect the look of the project as well as its lasting quality and even your ability to change the wallcovering later should you choose.

You can initially narrow down wallcovering options by considering the practicality and durability of various materials. Scrubbable and washable vinyls are great for high-moisture, high-use areas such as bathrooms, hallways, kids' rooms, and kitchens. Naturals such as grass cloth would be bad choices for those areas because they absorb dirt, moisture, and grease like a sponge. So before you start picking patterns, decide what is the best available material for the application.

Choosing a Wallcovering

To me, the most difficult part of a wallcovering job is choosing which to use. Seriously, you look at so many patterns and colors it's hard to keep them straight. Wallcovering manufacturers help you in your search by organizing groups of wallcoverings into collections. A collection is just that: a number of different patterns, each often executed in several color schemes, along with complementary materials and effects such as borders, wainscoting, and even murals.

Through the Looking Glass

Collections are sometimes organized around the design ideas of fashion designers and brands. Vera Wang, Ralph Lauren, and Eddie Bauer are some who offer wallcovering collections. And they have lots of company. So if you're fond of the work of a particular designer, ask your wallcovering retailer if that designer is represented in any collections.

Some wallcovering collections are licensed by media and entertainment companies. Disney, NASCAR (racing), NHL and NFL (pro sports), Nike (sportswear), and many other brand names offer licensed wallcovering collections. So you can cover the walls with your favorite team's logo or your kids' rooms with characters and scenes from their favorite cartoons and movies.

Impact

A decorating job often starts with the flooring. Per decorating dollar, however, you get far more impact with wallcoverings than with flooring. Flooring is more expensive than wallcovering but covers only one of six surfaces in a room. Wallcovering is on four others—all five of the others if the ceiling is covered. Wallcoverings are displayed at eye level, too, while the flooring is under your feet—and often under area rugs and large furnishings. So before you spend a big portion of your decorating budget on a surface that soils the fastest and is most likely to be hidden from view, consider spending some of it on wallcoverings—the results could be dramatic.

Collections are shown at wallcovering retailers in bound volumes called *wallpaper books*, *sample books*, or simply *collections*. These hefty tomes represent a significant investment on the part of wallcovering manufacturers—the industry spends $1 million or more per collection creating and photographing roomlike settings to demonstrate what the coverings look like when applied in a furnished, accessorized room, and printing and binding the books.

Because the books are costly and so there will be enough books available for all customers to review, most wallcovering retailers limit the number of books a customer can take home to study. Some retailers do not allow books to be taken out of the store. Dealers who do loan books will probably require a deposit that is refundable when you return the book. There's also usually a time limit on these loans—often 10 days.

SYMBOLS: International performance symbols like these often appear in wallcovering books and on product labels.

Symbol	Name	Symbol	Name
	Spongeable		Nonpasted
	Washable		Paste-the-wall
	Extra washable		Random match
	Scrubbable		Straight match
	Moderate light fastness		Drop match
	Good light fastness	$\frac{50}{25}$ cm	The repeat
	Strippable		Direction
	Peelable		Reverse hanging
	Prepasted		

Collections are generally organized into groups, often by room function. A wallcovering outlet might have several shelves of books devoted to living room collections and more shelves for dining rooms, kitchens, bathrooms, children's bedrooms, and more. These categories help you winnow down the vast number of patterns quickly. The categories are simply suggestions, however, and are not designed to limit you. If you see a pattern you like in a living room book and think it would be perfect in your bedroom, go ahead and use it! But be careful what kind of wallcoverings you apply to bathroom and kitchen walls—some materials will not stand up to high-moisture, high-traffic areas.

Anatomy of a Wallcovering Book

Collection

Photo

Border

Book

Colorway

Pattern

COLLECTION
Everything offered in a given book.

PATTERN
The basic graphic design of the covering.

COLORWAY
The colors in which the pattern is executed. One pattern is often available in many different colorways.

COMPLEMENTARY MATERIALS AND EFFECTS
Borders, wainscoting, and murals that coordinate with different wallcovering patterns. These are designed to enhance or complement the main pattern. They also can stand on their own: You can use a wallpaper border, for instance, as a frieze at the top of a painted wall.

VIGNETTE PHOTOGRAPHY
Photographs of the wallcovering installed in studio settings that bring the material to life in a homelike environment.

Wizards Plan Ahead
When you find a wallcovering you like in a book, you usually order it through the dealer to be delivered to your home by mail or express service. Orders often arrive in three to five days.

But before you set a date for applying the covering—or book a wallcovering contractor's time—make sure the material isn't back-ordered and that it will arrive before you need it.

USING THE BOOK

When you consider a sample in a wallcovering book, hold it vertically. That's how the material will be applied to the wall, and many materials will not look right viewed any other way. Slowly change the angle of a wallcovering book and you will probably see colors change, textures become more or less evident, and sheen and contrast vary as well. So it's important to view the material as it will be installed in your room, particularly with moiré or refractory patterns. After the pattern is printed, these materials are embossed with a texture that acts like a prism to reflect light in a specific manner. This quality is called *visual luster*.

Once you've narrowed your selection, ask if you can take the book—or a cut sample of the product—to the room where you're planning to apply it. Attach the sample to the wall with pushpins or blue painter's tape and look at it in morning, midday, afternoon, and evening light, and by artificial light. If the store has the wallcovering in stock, ask the retailer if you can take one roll home, handle it carefully, retain the labeling and packaging, and return it if you are not happy with this light test.

The Decorating Pyramid

Many people who attend my wallcovering workshops ask, "Where do I start decorating?" My answer is always to start your planning with the least changeable design element in a room and work toward the easiest to change. So build your decorating project from the ground up. Consider first the carpet or floor covering. Then move up to the wallcoverings and fabrics based on the flooring choices you've made. Continue up the pyramid until you reach paint—the easiest and least expensive of all the design elements to change.

With your plan complete it's time to get to work. When you're actually installing the design scheme, work from the other direction: the top down. Start with the paint and work your way through the other design elements in the room.

PAINT

When all other design elements are present, choose the appropriate color to apply to any painted walls, woodwork, and architectural detailing.

ACCESSORIES

Accessories such as collectibles and displays add personality and style to a room.

LIGHTING

Some lighting is permanent or fixed; other lighting, such as lamp lighting, mood lighting, display or art lighting, and undercounter lighting, can highlight areas, collections, or items of interest. It can also add dimension and mood to a room.

ARTWORK

Artwork reflects a sense of style and adds personality to a room.

FURNITURE

Furniture is expensive to replace, but rearranging pieces can give a room a completely different look. The style of furniture creates a particular atmosphere.

WALLCOVERINGS AND FABRICS

Coordinate wallcoverings and fabrics for upholstery and drapes with flooring. Wallcoverings and fabrics with a design and pattern give you a built-in selection of dominant and accent colors that act as the foundation for the rest of your design scheme.

FLOORING

Choose carpeting, wood, tile, vinyl, or linoleum floors first. These are big-ticket items that are expensive and time-consuming to change. A neutral shade gives you the most flexibility in your design plan; a pattern or colorful floor enlivens a room.

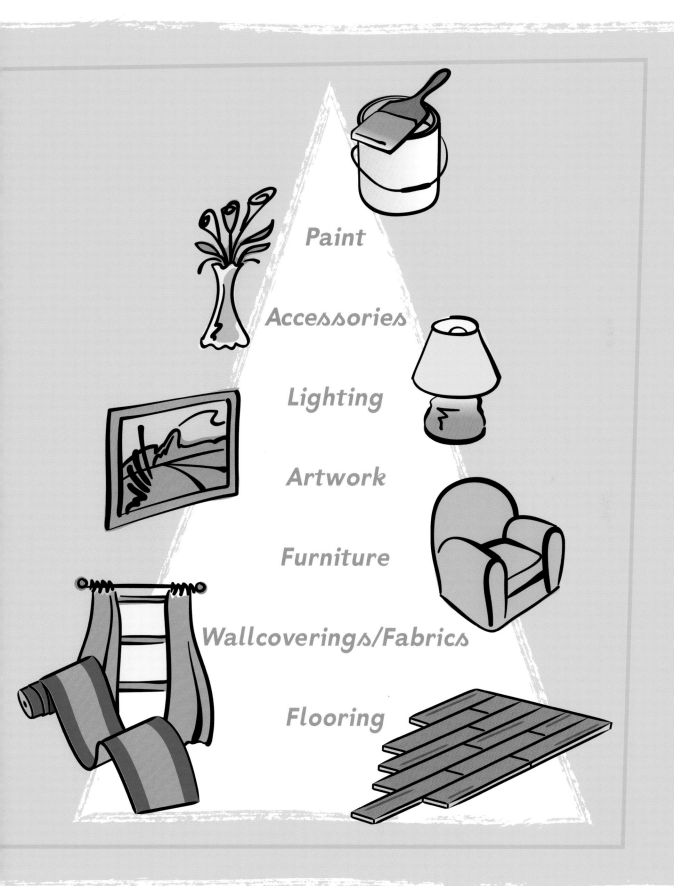

Paint

Accessories

Lighting

Artwork

Furniture

Wallcoverings/Fabrics

Flooring

Anatomy of a Wallcovering Design

REPEAT

Repeat is the distance between like elements of the design. Repeat differs from scale (opposite page) but is just as important because repeat determines the rhythm of the pattern. A long repeat will occur fewer times in a given space than a short repeat. The short repeat is more rhythmic because it repeats more often and the repetitions are more apparent. Whether a pattern has a short or long repeat is in itself neither good nor bad—suitability depends upon the room, how it will be furnished, and what effect you want to achieve.

LINE

Pattern repeats create lines in the wallcovering (except for solid-color wallcoverings with no pattern or texture). Some lines are obvious, as in a vertical stripe pattern, and others are more subtle, as in a floral or damask pattern. To see even the most subtle lines, stand back from the pattern and relax your eyes' focus. You may see vertical lines, horizontal lines, or diagonal lines, depending on the pattern. Sometimes you may see all three. Line is an important design element because your eye tends to follow a line. If the vertical line in the pattern is strongest, it can make a room seem taller. A horizontal line can make a room seem wider or longer; a diagonal line can make a room seem larger in every dimension.

STRAIGHT MATCH

DROP MATCH

RANDOM MATCH

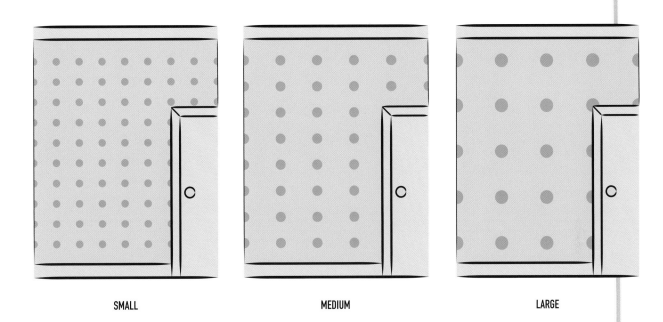

SMALL   MEDIUM   LARGE

SCALE

Scale is the size of the dominant element in the wallcovering's pattern. Some wallcovering designs have a large scale and some have a small scale, with infinite variations in between. The degree of contrast in the design, its colors, and the nature of the pattern itself all play a part in creating the overall effect. Other factors being equal designs of large scale tend to be more dramatic and those of a smaller scale are more intimate.

PROPORTION

Proportion is the ratio of the size of the dominant element within the wallcovering's pattern to the size of the room in which it's installed. Some ratios are naturally pleasing to the eye, while others are not. There are no absolutes—much depends on the shape of the room, its size, and the pattern and color of the wallcovering. Consider the pattern and judge how it will look in the room—whether the pattern is so large it will overwhelm a small room or so small it will appear busy in a large one.

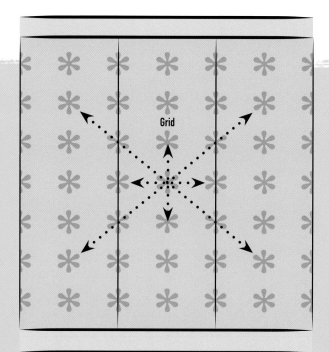

STRAIGHT MATCH

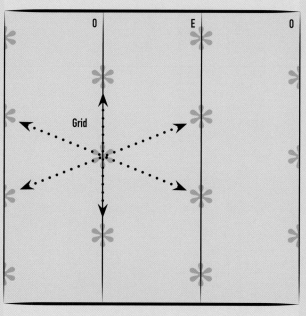

DROP MATCH

GRID

GRID stands for Greater Rhythm In Design, an acronym I coined long ago. It has since been adopted by the wallcovering industry to describe the interaction of scale, repeat, and line. Step back from an installed wallcovering, blur your focus, and you can see a literal grid in the design—intersecting horizontal, vertical, and at times diagonal lines that make up the wallcovering's metapattern, the big pattern behind all the smaller design elements. Ultimately it's GRID that determines the effect of the wallcovering in a given room, and the term provides an easy way to talk about all the elements of a wallcovering in one word.

Anatomy of a Bolt

A bolt is a continuous length of wallcovering rolled for convenient handling:

European Standard Bolts (Euro rolls) are 20½ inches wide and about 35 feet long and cover approximately 56 gross square feet (not including pattern repeat and pattern waste).

American Standard Bolts are approximately 27 inches wide and about 33 feet long and cover approximately 72 gross square feet (not including pattern repeat and pattern waste).

SPECIALTY BOLTS

• Borders usually range from 2 to 28 inches wide and are 15 feet long. Borders can also be packaged in a single continuous roll cut to a length you special order. They can be either straight runs with parallel edges or what's referred to as scallop- or laser-cut borders (right).

• Natural materials such as grass cloth are usually 36 inches wide and 24 feet long and cover about 72 gross square feet. Because natural materials tend to have grain, like wood, rather than the pattern of printed wallcoverings, the greater width is designed to create more of a panel effect—similar to wood paneling—than a pattern effect.

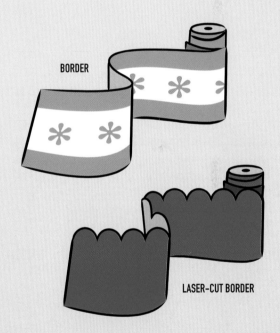

BORDER

LASER-CUT BORDER

Borders Without Borders

Designers have a new option these days: laser- or die-cut borders. Now they can create a pattern with an irregular edge that overlays the design of the wallcovering underneath, giving a frieze effect. These materials are usually applied directly over the wallcovering with a vinyl-over-vinyl adhesive. See pages 158–161 for examples of such borders.

How Many Rolls to Buy

Wallcoverings are priced and measured by the single roll, although they come packaged in double- or triple-roll bolts. Remember this as you figure out how much wallcovering to buy.

Today most wallcoverings come in Euro rolls, which hold about 25 percent less material than American rolls. However, most natural materials, such as grass cloth, cork, bamboo, and burlap, are sold by the American roll. Determine whether the material you are buying is measured in Euro (metric) rolls or American (nonmetric) rolls. Then estimate the number of rolls to buy as follows:

Multiply the perimeter of the room (the length of all walls added together) by the height of the room (the distance from floor to ceiling, including moldings, if any). The result is the gross square footage of the walls. If you'll be applying Euro rolls and the ceilings are less than 9 feet high, divide the gross square footage by 25—the number of usable square feet in a Euro roll. If the room is taller than 9 feet, divide by 23.5. This lower number accounts for the added height of the room and increased pattern repeat usage in the roll.

If you are buying American rolls, divide the gross square footage by 27 for rooms less than 9 feet tall, divide by 25.5 for rooms more than 9 feet tall. Don't deduct any square footage for doors and windows; that helps to ensure you have enough material to account for trimming waste, pattern repeat, and pattern match.

Order at least one more bolt than you think you'll need. You can always return it if you don't use it, but trying to buy more wallcovering later with the same pattern and dye lot can be an exercise in frustration. And if the pattern has been discontinued or the stock of a dye lot exhausted, you'll have to strip what you've already applied and start over. Keep any extra wallcovering on hand for future repairs. It can also be handy for making room embellishments, such as covers for switchplates, heater vent grilles, or even lampshades, wastebaskets, or other decorative features.

How to order border

Borders are packaged in 15-foot or 5-yard lengths, so divide the perimeter of the room in feet by 15 to find the number of border packages you'll need. There's no way of knowing where the pattern starts on each roll, so always order at least one more package than you think you'll need. Order two more packages on larger jobs. That accounts for the amount of usable pattern repeat within each roll—and may even leave you some leftover material to use in creating other decorative effects.

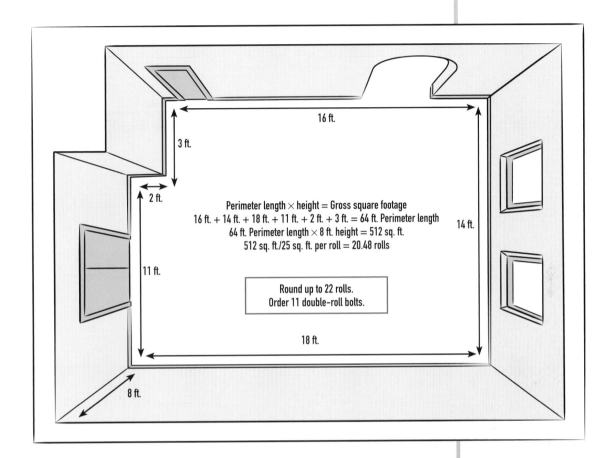

Perimeter length × height = Gross square footage
16 ft. + 14 ft. + 18 ft. + 11 ft. + 2 ft. + 3 ft. = 64 ft. Perimeter length
64 ft. Perimeter length × 8 ft. height = 512 sq. ft.
512 sq. ft./25 sq. ft. per roll = 20.48 rolls

Round up to 22 rolls.
Order 11 double-roll bolts.

MATERIAL ESTIMATION

When Is a Roll Not a Roll?

A roll is a unit of measure, just like a foot or a yard. It's not a physical roll of material, in spite of the name. The coiled cylinder of wallcovering material that you buy is called a bolt, like a bolt of fabric. Just as a bolt of fabric may contain many yards, a bolt of wallcovering almost always contains more than one roll of wallcovering. Most bolts contain two or three rolls of material in one continuous length. Thus a particular wallcovering that is sold in rolls that are 16 feet long may be packaged as a double-roll bolt, a continuous length 32 feet long rolled into a cylinder. So once you've determined how many rolls you need, find out how many rolls are in a bolt of the pattern you're buying. Then divide the number of rolls in your total by the number of rolls in a bolt to determine the number of packages—bolts—of wallcovering to buy.

The Material World

MATERIAL TYPE
Wallcoverings are available in five common materials.

• **Vinyl-coated materials** have a washable or scrubbable vinyl coating applied to the surface, either as an ingredient in the inks that create the pattern or as a clear coating over the top of a pattern, much like the clear coat on a car or the varnish on a hardwood floor. Vinyl-coated papers offer an ideal combination of price, stability, and ease of use.

• **Vinyl-laminated materials** are made of two layers: an outer layer of vinyl that has the pattern printed on it and a substrate, or paper backing, that adheres to the wall. They are easy to strip—you simply grab the vinyl layer and pull the whole layer off at once, as the adhesive that holds the vinyl layer to the paper layer is weaker than the adhesive that holds the paper layer to the wall. Then you strip the paper substrate separately, which is relatively easy because the paper has no ink or vinyl coating on it and readily absorbs stripping solution. These wallcoverings have largely been abandoned by the industry and are hard to find, although a few patterns are still available. They are very washable, so if you can find one, it would be great for a bath or kitchen.

Each of the five different types of wallcovering materials has its own characteristics.

• **Solid vinyl** is one solid sheet of vinyl that's extruded, colored, and applied to cheesecloth backing to which the adhesive can bond. Generally these are either nonpatterned or random-patterned and are scrubbable and extremely durable. They are excellent for commercial spaces. Solid-vinyl wallcoverings are installed frequently in large commercial buildings such as hotels and convention centers.

• **Naturals** are organic materials such as grass cloth, cork, or bamboo that are laminated to a heavy paper backing for stability. Natural materials tend to be expensive, and most are not washable, but they create an effect that you simply can't get with a printed material.

• **Untrimmed materials** date back to the 1400s, when patterns were printed on paper stock using hand-cut wooden blocks. Up to 30 different colors might be used to create a single design. You can still buy a few historic patterns made with this material. They're costly and most often used in historic restoration projects. These papers require hand-trimming before applying.

Nonwovens

The wallcovering of the future is beginning to hit the market. These nonwoven materials are infused with an adhesive on one side and a pattern on the other. A single sheet includes the adhesive, the backing, the decorative face, the pattern, and the washable surface all in one. These materials are extremely washable and durable. The pattern penetrates into the surface of the material, giving a dimensional quality that conventionally printed coverings don't have.

The adhesives penetrate the base material, creating a consistency of adhesion. They are also 100 percent strippable: If you don't like the pattern in five years, you can grab it and pull everything off the wall in one swoop—pattern, substrate, adhesive, and all. Nonwovens are also very stable materials, so seams stay straight and are virtually invisible.

Anatomy of a Sheet

Here's where the wallcovering hits the wall—in the form of a sheet. A sheet is the most basic element of a wallcovering job, just as a brick is the most basic element of a brick wall.

SHEET

A length of wallcovering cut to the height of the wall to be covered plus 4 inches (see page 108).

KEY ELEMENT

The largest obvious graphic element printed on the face of the wallcovering.

Some wallcoverings such as textures, naturals, and random match designs have no key element, but they do have shade variations (see page 120).

PATTERN REPEAT

The interval between reoccurrences of the key element, usually 1 to 36 inches.

BACKING OR SUBSTRATE

The side of the material on which the adhesive is applied.

TRIM-OFF

The part of the material removed to allow the wallcovering to fit the wall.

BORDER

A narrow strip of wallcovering that complements the main design.

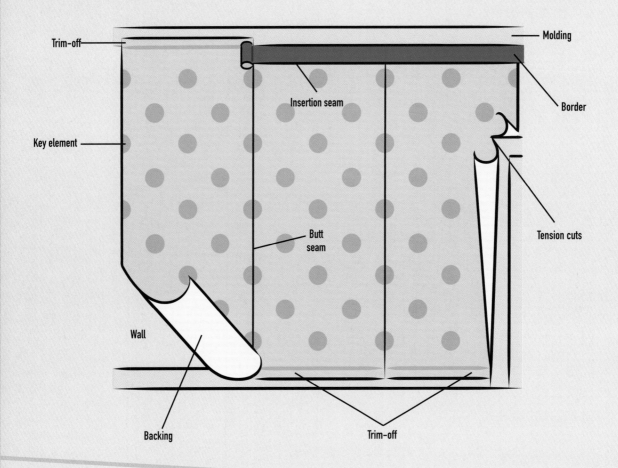

Trim-off • Molding • Key element • Insertion seam • Border • Butt seam • Tension cuts • Wall • Backing • Trim-off

Same pattern, same place

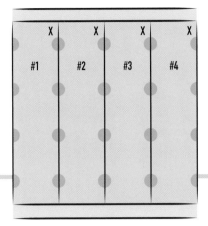

STRAIGHT MATCH

The pattern lines up horizontally.

Every other sheet matches

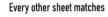

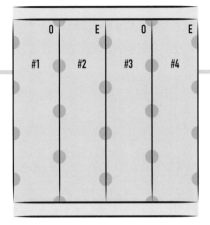

DROP MATCH

The pattern lines up diagonally as well as horizontally.

Reverse-hanging for shading

RANDOM MATCH

Pattern elements do not align horizontally or diagonally.

SEAMS

BUTT SEAM

Where two sheets of wallcovering meet edge to edge without cutting or trimming. See previous page.

INSERTION SEAM

Where two materials overlap, such as a border and a wallcovering. See previous page.

DOUBLE-CUT SEAM

Where two sheets overlap and a single cut is made through both layers. The trim-off is removed, resulting in a perfect butt seam as shown at right.

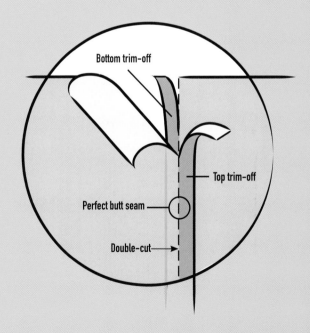

Bottom trim-off

Top trim-off

Perfect butt seam

Double-cut

The Sticky Stuff

Over the past two decades, there has been a great deal of experimentation with adhesives, some more successful than others. These days your adhesive options have been refined to a tried-and-true few:

ORGANIC ADHESIVES

Usually starch-based, these water-soluble adhesives have good tack, or holding power, but release when saturated, facilitating stripping. Their solubility makes them easy to work with so you can clean your tools, worktable, and the inevitable slops and spills easily. Organic adhesives also won't stain, so they're generally used on very fine papers such as murals and organics that might stain easily if synthetic adhesives are used.

BLENDED ADHESIVES

These adhesives blend organic and synthetic materials. They have greater bond strength than organic adhesives yet are still relatively easy to clean up.

SYNTHETIC ADHESIVES

Acrylic-based and extremely strong and tacky, synthetics are an excellent choice for use in kitchens, bathrooms, and other high-moisture areas where organic adhesives might fail. A synthetic bond can easily be sheared, making wallcoverings applied with this adhesive easily strippable. Adhesive drips and spills are hard to remove from room surfaces, and they're even more tenacious when they dry. Residual adhesive that's dried onto a wall is virtually impossible to remove and can impair surfaces to be painted. Organic or blended adhesives are a better choice in most cases.

Activators?

Activator, a gel-like material that absorbs and holds moisture, has become available in the last 10 years. It's designed to eliminate the need for wetting the wallcovering in a water tray to activate the adhesive. Instead you roll the activator gel onto the back of the wallcovering. It does work, but it takes more time and energy to roll the stuff onto the wallcovering thoroughly and evenly than to simply dunk the wallcovering in a tray the conventional way. In the Wizard's world activators are a tedious, tiring, and expensive extra step.

Sticky-Note Technology

Releasable or pressure-sensitive adhesives will become very popular in the next 20 years, I believe. Like stick-on notepads these adhesives allow a wallcovering to stick to a wall without any liquid application to the wallcovering or wall, making the process much less messy. When you want to strip the wallcovering, you just pull it off the wall, taking all adhesive residue with it. You can already buy borders—particularly trendy border designs for children's rooms—with this type of adhesive, allowing you to change a room's look easily to keep up with a growing child. But for now releasables are expensive and they're not available in full sheets.

PREPASTED WALLCOVERINGS

Wallcoverings with adhesive applied at the factory during the manufacturing process eliminate the need to apply adhesive to the paper during installation. That saves installation time and mess and provides a more consistent bond.

NONPASTED WALLCOVERINGS

Adhesive must be applied to some wallcoverings before you install them. Nonpasted wallcoverings take slightly more time to install but allow an experienced wallcovering installer to adjust the amount and consistency of the adhesive to match the porosity of the wall and the wallcovering backing.

Chapter 3

Preparation

The natural inclination with any project is to jump right in and start the work so you can see some results—preferably within a few hours. But take it from the Wall Wizard: The success of any home improvement project depends on preparation. And that's especially true for installing wallcoverings.

About 80 percent of the work done by any professional wallcovering contractor is preparation—not installation. All room surfaces must be prepped before wallcoverings can be installed; they must be scrubbed, repaired, and smoothed. You will put in 1 to 3 hours of prep time for every hour you spend actually applying the wallcoverings.

I know it sounds like drudgery and lots of work. And you know what—it is! But believe me, the time spent properly prepping a room will more than repay itself in a quicker, smoother, more professional job. Here's why:

☆ A clean, cleared-out room is safer and easier to work in than one cluttered with furnishings—and your work will go much faster too.

☆ Proper preparation avoids damaging floors, walls, woodwork, and built-ins both before and during the application process—and makes cleanup afterward easy.

☆ Clean, sound surfaces are the foundation for good adhesion, so wallcoverings are less likely to peel, curl, bubble, or discolor.

☆ Smooth surfaces ensure that when you're done, you'll see the wallcovering—not the imperfections underneath.

Rules of Tools

The first step is to gather the right tools for the job. Invest in the best. This doesn't mean the most expensive, but rather the most effective, tools. Consider these rules when purchasing tools:

Buy quality, not just price. Quality wears better and lasts longer.

Buy plastic or stainless-steel tools. They are unaffected by strippers and pastes. Because they don't rust they don't contaminate the materials you're working with, plus they're easy to clean and long-lasting.

Buy brightly colored tools. Fluorescent green, yellow, and orange tools are easier to spot in a work area and make it easier to avoid mishaps.

Buy plastic containers with airtight lids. Unbreakable and sealable containers are best for short- and long-term storage of wallcovering stripping solution and cleaning solutions.

Buy ergonomic tools. Big, comfortable grips promote better tool control and reduce muscle fatigue. Easy, stress-free work brings better results.

Tools:
Good and Bad

You'll find a lot of choices in tools. I've tried about every tool available and even invented a few of my own. Along the way I've found there are good tools and bad tools and that sometimes having the right tool can make the difference between a smooth job and a frustrating one. You don't need a lot of tools, but you do need the right ones for the job, and they need to be of good quality.

Marking Tools

GOOD
Pencils make layout marks on the wall that won't show through in the final job—and can be erased if you mismark.

BAD
Felt-tip markers and ink pens make marks that will bleed through wallcoverings.

Alignment Tools

GOOD
Plumb lines and laser lines give you perfectly vertical lines.

BAD
Levels are less accurate than plumb lines and laser lines and are harder to use.

Openers

GOOD
The 10-in-1 tool is designed to open a can of paint without damaging the can lid.

BAD
Can keys often damage the lip of the can, allowing air to get in and ruin the contents.

Knives

GOOD
Snap-blade knives are slender, lightweight, and brightly colored and allow you to use a fresh blade for every cut on wallcoverings.

BAD
Utility knives are larger, more cumbersome, and easier to lose, and require more time to change blades.

Sanding Tools

GOOD
Scouring pads are easy to rinse clean and long-lasting and can be used wet for practically dustless smoothing of spackle and drywall compound when repairing walls.

BAD
Traditional sanding blocks create dust, and the abrasive clogs easily and must be replaced often, adding expense and time to the job.

Seam Setting Tools

GOOD

The plastic float or seam smoother is comfortable in your hand, puts even pressure on the seam, and will not squeeze the adhesive out of the seam.

BAD

The seam roller applies too much pressure to the seam, leaving indentations in the wallcovering surface. It also squeezes out the adhesive, resulting in lifting seams.

Broad Knives

GOOD

A 4-inch broad knife makes an excellent guide when trimming wallcoverings after application and is small enough to fit in a work pouch.

BAD

An 8-inch broad knife is unwieldy to work with comfortably, blocks your vision as you're trimming, and reduces accuracy when cutting around irregular profiles such as moldings.

Ladders

GOOD

An aluminum platform ladder is lightweight and comfortable to stand on, allows you to get close to the wall, and offers a shelf to hold tools.

BAD

A 5-foot stepladder is heavy and uncomfortable to stand on and places you too far from the wall to work efficiently.

Smoothing Tools

GOOD

A wallcovering brush applies even pressure to the wallcovering when applying sheets to the wall and fits easily in your hand and tool pouch.

BAD

A sponge can drag the wallcovering out of alignment and mar the wallcovering surface.

Recommended Tools

Here are the tools I am never without. None of them is terribly expensive, so get good ones and they'll last almost forever. I've used many of my tools almost daily for at least 20 years, and they are still as good as new.

BUCKET TROLLEY

One of my inventions, this allows you to keep a bucket of primer, sealer, or fresh water for cleaning close at hand. Buy a large, round plastic planter base with casters and a length of 2-inch foam pipe insulation from a garden store or home center. Wrap the pipe insulation around the lip of the planter base for a bumper, and you have a bucket caddy that you can roll around the room with a gentle nudge of your toe when your hands are full of tools or other materials.

10-IN-1 TOOL

This is perhaps the ultimate wall worker's multitool. It has a comfort-grip handle, two screwdriver bits that fold out of the back, a hammering surface, and a nail puller. The point on the blade can dig out old caulk, open up cracks for spackling, or punch holes in paint can rims so the paint drains back into the can. It also has a scraper head for removing wallcovering and old paint, a putty knife edge for filling nail holes in wallboard or plaster with spackle, and a curved edge for cleaning paint from a roller. You can even open cans of paint or spackle with the square bumpout on the side of the blade. You don't want to be without one of these!

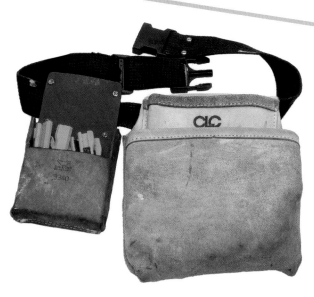

WALLPAPER SMOOTHING BRUSH

This is the oldest and most indispensable wallcovering application tool. Buy a 12-inch-long bright-colored plastic one that's easy to find and clean. With two passes it can cover the width of a sheet of wallcovering, allowing you to work quickly. The bristles act like hundreds of little fingers that massage the air from beneath the paper, creating a vacuum that holds the covering to the wall until the adhesive starts to set. The bristles apply pressure evenly so they don't damage the material or stretch it out of shape. You can also tamp a seam into place with the bristles before you smooth it down.

TOOL POUCH

A large leather pouch holds tools as you work. Leather is soft and flexible, so it doesn't impede mobility, yet it's tough enough to allow you to snap off snap-blade knife tips inside the pouch, which then safely contains the tips. The pouch has a belt of nylon webbing that's lightweight, comfortable, and easy to put on and take off with a quick-release buckle.

TRIMMING GUARDS

A 4-inch broad knife fits in your tool pouch. Use it to gently hold the wallcovering securely against the wall so it doesn't move when you trim away the waste. Its metal blade protects the wallcovering underneath from knife slips yet is small enough to work around irregular surfaces accurately. The 12- and 24-inch guards have long, straight stainless-steel blades that are used as straightedge guides for ensuring that you make a perfectly straight cut when cutting borders and double-cutting seams.

CHALKLINE

Plastic-bodied, brightly colored, and filled with nonstaining yellow chalk, this chalkline is small enough to fit into a tool pouch and allows you to snap a perfectly straight plumb line from floor to ceiling. A nice big pushpin is easy to insert into and remove from the wall and gives the line something to hang from.

FLOAT

A wallcovering float fits comfortably in your hand. You use it to set seams with light up and down strokes. You can also use a float to gently remove bubbles from beneath wallcovering while the adhesive is still wet by pulling it slowly toward you over the bubble. Never push the tool forward because it can plow or gouge into the surface.

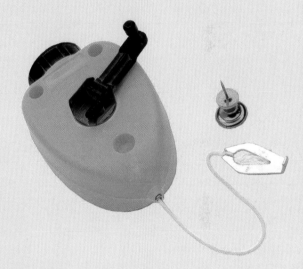

LASER LEVEL

This high-tech alternative to the plumb line and chalkline throws a perfectly straight, unwavering beam of colored light over a considerable distance and eliminates the need to climb a ladder and stick a pushpin in the wall. It's a timesaver when working on particularly large or tall surfaces, such as in stairwells or rooms with cathedral ceilings. It also allows you to create a perfectly horizontal line—making it a great tool to have when installing borders—without the chalk residue.

Task-Grouped Tools

Wallcovering application is a multistep process, so you will use different tools at different stages. Here they are grouped by project stage. As you begin each operation, refer to this page to see which tools to gather.

LAYOUT TOOLS

These tools are used for creating the layout, the first step in any wallcovering job. You'll use a **tape measure** for measuring the room, a **pencil** for marking your layout on the walls, and a **notepad** for recording the number and length of each sheet.

PROCESSING TOOLS

You'll use this group of tools to process the wallcoverings—to precut and label the sheets before activating the adhesive and applying them to the wall. **Framing squares** are used as cutting guides to make perfectly square, straight cuts, both when slicing through the material with a **snap-blade knife** and when tearing the material directly against the square's edge. **Aluminum squares** don't rust and are light and easy to handle; **steel squares** are heavier and handy for keeping materials that tend to curl flat on your layout table. **Scissors** offer an alternative method for cutting wallcoverings; **cutting guides** are great for cutting angled sheets for stairwells or slanted ceilings. **Rubber bands** secure back-rolled materials in their rolled form. **Spring clamps** are useful anytime you need an extra hand, such as when applying adhesive to borders. Fasten clamps to the table with **duct tape.**

PASTING TOOLS

An **activation tray** facilitates activation of the adhesive on prepasted wallcoverings. I use a flower box—it's made of tough ABS plastic that won't split, crack, or shatter and holds 3½ gallons of water. Nonpasted wallcoverings require a **paint roller** and either a foam- or fiber-nap **roller cover,** a **paint roller tray,** and **adhesive.** A **border applicator** applies adhesive to borders and comes preloaded with adhesive. Kitchen- or trash-compactor-size plastic **trash bags** prevent the pasted or activated wallcoverings from drying out while they're being transported and are waiting to be applied to the wall; the bags are used for job cleanup later. An **oversize indelible marker** marks the trash bags— not the wallcovering sheets themselves—with the numbers of the sheets inside.

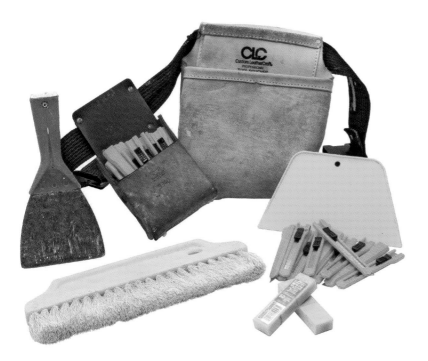

INSTALLATION TOOLS

A **tool pouch** keeps tools at hand while you work, saving time and energy. A **slider pouch** holds **snap-blade knives** for trimming wallcoverings after they've been applied to the wall. The larger pouch holds additional knives, boxes of **knife blade refills,** a **wallpaper smoothing brush** for applying wallcoverings to the wall, a **4-inch broad knife,** and a **plastic float.** The large pouch also provides a safe place to snap off used blade tips and contain them until they can be discarded safely. The total cost of these tools is less than that of a cordless drill; but with the exception of the expendable knife blades, they'll last you a lifetime.

Cleaning Tools

Keep various sizes of **plastic trash bags** and **resealable plastic bags** handy for storing hardware and switchplates. For dusty cleanup tasks, a **shop vacuum cleaner,** a **push broom** with **dustpan,** and a **dusting brush** will come in handy. You'll need **5-gallon buckets**, clean-rinsing **tile sponges,** a sponge-head **floor mop** with nylon scrubbing pads, and a nylon-bristle **deck brush** with **extension pole. Large household sponges** with a nylon scrubbing pad, **2-quart plastic buckets,** and lots of **terry cloth towels** will round out your cleaning supplies.

Solvents

A solvent is a substance used to dissolve other materials. Solvents are described as cold, warm, or hot according to their degree of volatility, chemical makeup, and use. Your selection of cleaning solutions should be based on the surface and the type of cleaning you need to do.

Cold. Water is nature's solvent. Water-base cleaning products, such as trisodium phosphate (TSP), ammonia, hydrogen peroxide, and all-purpose cleaners, remove dirt and are neutralized with distilled white vinegar. These products are people-safe and earth-friendly.

Warm. When a moderate cleaning material is needed, denatured alcohol, acetone, muriatic acid, and rubbing alcohol all work well. These products are effective surface cleaners, but be sure to rinse well. They are safe when handled, stored, and disposed of properly.

Hot. Petroleum-base products such as mineral spirits or paint thinners are hot solvents formulated to break down the chemistry of oily substances. Naphtha, turpentine, and lacquer thinner are other hot solvents. Protect yourself and handle these materials with caution. Use, store, and dispose of these hazardous materials properly. Neutralize the surfaces these solvents have been applied to by wiping them down with denatured alcohol.

CLEANING CHEMICALS

Wear heavy-duty gloves and eye protection for safety. **TSP** is an alkaline cleaner that dissolves grease and deglosses surfaces. To kill mold and mildew, use hydrogen peroxide. Use an **ammonia-base** or **alkaline household cleaner** for removing dirt and white vinegar as a mild acid-rinsing agent. As a base material, baking soda can neutralize an acid. Citrus-base cleaners, such as Goof Off 2, work especially well. Rubbing alcohol can clean grease, grime, dirt, and other organic spots from metal hardware. When working with volatile chemicals, use nonflammable shop rags that are coated to prevent spontaneous combustion.

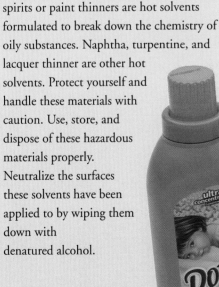

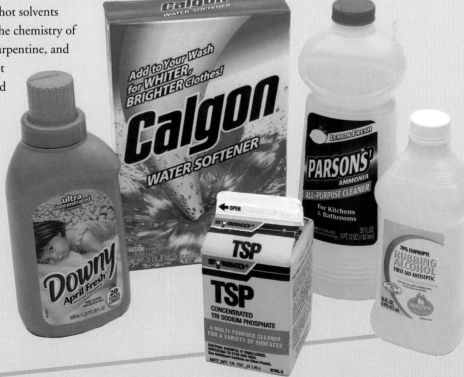

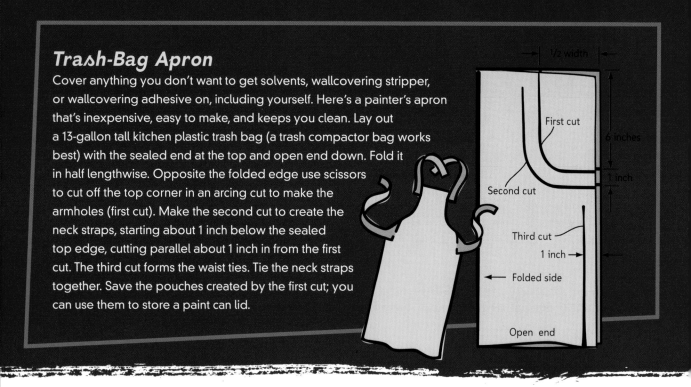

Trash-Bag Apron

Cover anything you don't want to get solvents, wallcovering stripper, or wallcovering adhesive on, including yourself. Here's a painter's apron that's inexpensive, easy to make, and keeps you clean. Lay out a 13-gallon tall kitchen plastic trash bag (a trash compactor bag works best) with the sealed end at the top and open end down. Fold it in half lengthwise. Opposite the folded edge use scissors to cut off the top corner in an arcing cut to make the armholes (first cut). Make the second cut to create the neck straps, starting about 1 inch below the sealed top edge, cutting parallel about 1 inch in from the first cut. The third cut forms the waist ties. Tie the neck straps together. Save the pouches created by the first cut; you can use them to store a paint can lid.

1/2 width

First cut

6 inches

1 inch

Second cut

Third cut

1 inch

Folded side

Open end

Protective Clothing

Your body is a giant sponge, and you can absorb chemicals through your skin. To protect yourself wear nonporous **vinyl gloves.** Latex gloves tear easily and are porous, allowing some chemicals to seep through. Sprinkle baby powder into the gloves so they slip on more easily. Wrap a piece of **masking tape** around the cuff to seal it. For full protection put on **disposable paper coveralls** and **painter's hat** or **shower cap** (or even a **food-storage cover**). Wear **goggles, safety glasses,** or a **face shield** to protect your eyes from dust, chips, or solvents; a **dust mask** filters out dust; a **respirator** protects you from dust and chemical fumes.

Trash-bag apron

Food-storage covers

Respirator

Painter's hat

Dust mask

Dust mask

Safety glasses

Shower cap

Vinyl gloves

Protecting the Room

Pretaped **masking film** combines masking tape and plastic sheeting in a roll-out dispenser. The film unfolds to about 24 inches, providing a drop cloth that protects surrounding surfaces from spills and splatters. The film is biodegradable, so you can throw it away with the trash. Instead of buying a big, heavy tarp like the pros use, purchase a **disposable paper/plastic drop cloth.** Face the paper side up to absorb spills and the plastic side down to protect a surface. This product is nonslip so you won't go sliding across it, and it is biodegradable, so you can wad it up and toss it in the trash when you are finished.

Protect furniture and other items that are too big to move with **9×12-foot, .7-mil plastic sheeting.** It provides a lot of coverage and is inexpensive and biodegradable, so you can throw it away when you're finished. It does have one drawback—it is hard to unfold. Here's a trick: Place the plastic, still in the package, in the freezer for about 30 minutes. This removes the static charge on the plastic, so when you take it out, it's easy to unfold.

If you immediately lay it out over furniture, it will cling to the furniture as it warms up. And here's one more tip: Don't use old bedsheets or newspapers to protect surfaces when you apply wallcovering. Wallcovering stripper and wallcovering adhesive will go right through them, damaging the surface beneath.

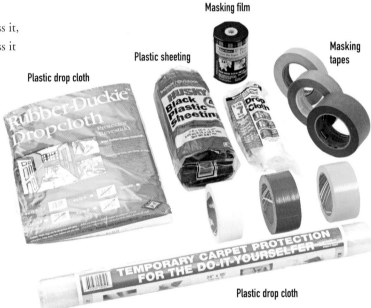

Masking film

Plastic sheeting

Masking tapes

Plastic drop cloth

Plastic drop cloth

Baby Wipes

Baby wipes are a great $2 solution for cleanup. Think about it: These wipes are designed to clean up really messy messes. The alcohol in the wipes removes grease, grime, and dirt without leaving a residue on the wall. If you use the wipes as a cleaner for hot solvents, the lanolin in the wipes stops the photochemical reaction in the solvents that can cause spontaneous combustion. The wipes are biodegradable, and they smell better than dirty old rags.

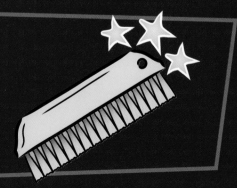

Caulking and Patching Tools

Get a **caulking gun** and a tube of **white water-base acrylic caulk** to fill larger gaps and cracks and a damp sponge to smooth the caulk. Spackle, wallboard joint compound, or patching plaster will fill holes and cracks in the walls; 6-inch and 10-inch broad knives smooth patching compound. A 2-inch putty knife and paint scrapers will prove useful during preparation. Home centers and hardware stores sell a number of ready-to-use patching compounds in handy dispensers. My favorite is a **Patch Stick:** Dab a bit of the filler onto the wall, then smooth it with the straightedge on the head of the stick. A **10-in-1 tool** is perhaps the ultimate wall worker's multitool. It has a comfort-grip handle; two screwdriver bits that fold out of the back of the tool; a hammering surface on the butt of the handle; a teardrop-shape nail puller; a point that can dig out old caulk, open up cracks for spackling, or punch holes in paint can rims so the paint drains back into the can and the lid fits securely; a scraper head for removing wallcovering and old paint; a putty knife edge for filling nail holes in wallboard or plaster with spackle; and a curved edge for cleaning paint from a roller. You can even open cans of paint or patching compound with the square bumpout on the side of the blade. You don't want to be without one of these!

Sanding Tools

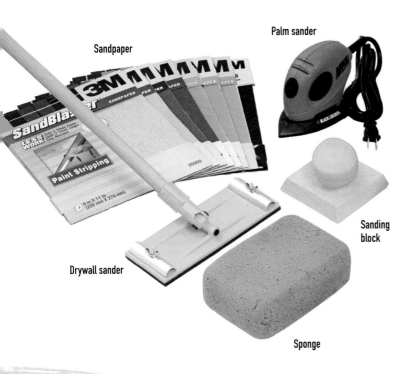

Sandpaper

Palm sander

Sanding block

Drywall sander

Sponge

Use **sandpaper** grits from 60 to 220 for patching and repair. A **sanding block** is good to smooth a patching job; a **palm sander** or half-sheet orbital sander works nicely as well. A **drywall sander** uses a nonclogging abrasive screen rather than sandpaper, and it has an extension pole for high or hard-to-reach places. Some versions can be hooked to a shop vacuum, allowing you to suck up the dust before it spreads and settles around the room. Some dust is inevitable; a damp **sponge** helps remove it from room surfaces. If heavy sanding is required, use a respirator.

Wallcovering Removal Tools

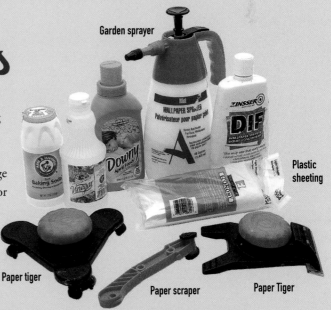

Garden sprayer

Plastic sheeting

Paper tiger

Paper scraper

Paper Tiger

Removing wallcovering requires a few tools. Use a broom handle to roll strippable wallcoverings off the wall. A rolling mop bucket reduces back strain. It is also a hands-free tool you can move with your foot. A **trigger-spray plastic garden sprayer** quickly applies wallcovering remover to large areas. Buy a new sprayer; don't use one that has been used for herbicides or pesticides. A **Paper Tiger** is a handy tool that perforates wallcovering and makes it easier to remove. A **paper scraper** with a wide, flat edge angled so that it easily lifts wallcovering from the surface is essential. You will also need **baking soda, fabric softener,** and **wallcovering remover concentrate** with enzymes to make the proper potion for wallcovering removal. Stir 1 cup of **vinegar** into 1 gallon of water to rinse walls. Have several clean 5-gallon buckets on hand, along with plenty of **.7-mil plastic sheeting** to cover the walls from top to bottom. Use heavier sheeting and duct tape to protect floors from moisture and old towels to absorb excess water.

Drywall Repair Tools

You will need fiberglass mesh reinforcing tape and **quick-drying plaster compound** for medium-size holes. For large holes have a drywall saw, scraps of drywall, moistened paper joint tape, oil-base sealer, and wallboard screws on hand. To drive the fasteners you'll want a **corded or cordless drill driver** (cordless models are more convenient). You'll also need a tape measure, a utility knife, and a drywall square or carpenter's square to measure and cut the drywall. For convenience in mixing large buckets of joint compound, chuck a **mixing auger** into your drill. **Taping knives** smooth the drywall compound after your patch is applied. The **10-in-1 tool** performs myriad tasks related to drywall work—see pages 53 and 62 for more information on how this tool can help you work faster and better.

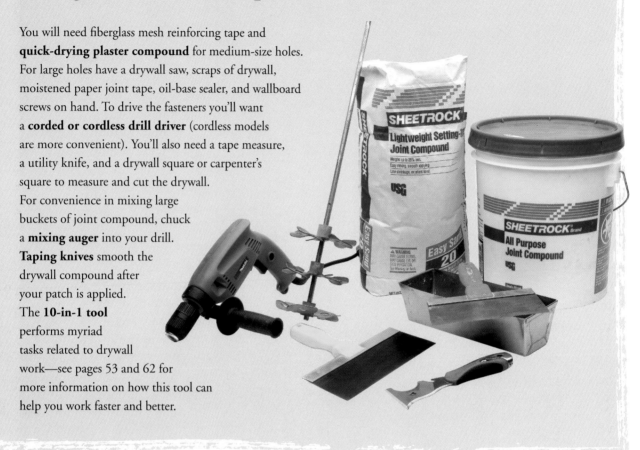

BUCKET BRIGADE

Bucket stilts help you reach higher with ease (see page 65 for how to make your own). A **trash bucket** with a **plastic bag liner** is essential for capturing debris; a **bungee cord** keeps the liner from sliding into the bucket, and a **bucket trolley** (see page 53) allows you to roll it around the room with a nudge of your toe. **Buckets** hold water for rinsing down wallcoverings after application; **towels** dry the rinsed wallcoverings, preventing spotting.

Extend Your Reach

5-FOOT PLATFORM LADDER

A **lightweight aluminum ladder,** below left, is my choice for giving you a step up in the world. Its sturdy yet simple design allows you to directly face the wall while you work. It weighs only 10 pounds, so you can easily close it with one hand by lifting up the built-in shelf, and it also folds 3 inches flat for storage. When opened it has two steps: The upper one is a 12×18-inch platform, which is easier to stand on than a standard ladder rung and brings you comfortably within reach of an 8-foot ceiling. The ladder has a built-in safety cage, and it is wide enough to bridge over a toilet but narrow enough to place into a bathtub. It's much better than a **conventional stepladder,** such as the one shown at right. Conventional ladders like these have skinny steps that are fatiguing to stand on, lack a safety cage, keep you farther away from the wall surface you're working on, and are heavy and cumbersome to move and set up.

If you have a high ceiling or stairwell, you might need scaffolding. You can rent scaffolding from most equipment rental outlets. The easiest type to use has locking wheels and folds for transport or storage. Look for the type that is narrow enough to roll through a standard doorway. A multiladder can be configured as a 16-foot straight ladder, a 4- or 8-foot-tall stepladder, 4-foot-high and 8-foot-long scaffolding, a standoff ladder, and a stair ladder. Available at home centers and hardware stores, it's a great combination tool that comes in handy for chores both inside and out.

GOOD

BAD

Bucket Stilts

Bucket stilts make it easy to reach the top of a wall. Buy two 5-gallon paint buckets with lids. Trace your shoe outline on each lid and mark the attachment points at the toe and heel. Attach double-sided hook-and-loop straps to the lids with machine bolts, fender washers, and nylon locknuts. Secure as shown. Glue a large rubber pad to the bottom of each bucket to prevent slipping. Voilá!

My Mistake!

Yee-Ow!

TWO PEOPLE CAN BE STUPID AT THE SAME TIME
SO TRIPLE YOUR SAFETY PRECAUTIONS.

I used to turn off all the light switches in a room before working there, then turn off the power at the breaker box. "That way," I thought, "I'm doubly protected." True enough, but sometimes double just isn't enough.

Once after my partner and I had finished applying wallcoverings in a master suite, I was reinstalling the lights in a bathroom while my partner was reattaching the outlets and switchplates in the adjoining bedroom. He finished first and went to the breaker box to turn the bedroom power back on. He inadvertently restored the current to the bathroom as well.

Not good, but not horrible either. He'd defeated only one of my safety precautions, and so far, no current to the wires.

Then, just as I was attaching the last two wires together with a wire nut, he walked into the bathroom and flipped the switch on.

Yee-ow! wasn't all I had to say about it.

Lesson learned:
Use as many safety precautions as you can. Now I turn off the switch, turn off the circuit breaker, and tape the switch in the "off" position.

Ready the Room

An empty room is an easy place to apply wallcovering, so begin by removing everything you can from the room. Gather anything that is left to one side of the room, away from your work area.

Turn off the power to any outlets or fixtures on the walls or ceiling you'll be working on. Then remove all light fixtures, switchplates and outlet plates, heat register covers, towel rods, drapes (get them cleaned while they are down), and drapery hardware. Don't try to apply wallcovering around the hardware; it is too frustrating and time-consuming. Pay particular attention to how your window treatments are attached and make a diagram, if necessary, so you can reinstall them correctly and without guesswork.

If you're going to be applying wallcovering to a ceiling (see page 150 for more information), loosen the canopy or trim piece of a ceiling fixture or chandelier and slide it down the fixture away from the ceiling. Wrap it with plastic trash bags or plastic wrap. Never unscrew a fixture from the electrical box and allow it to hang by its wires—the wires aren't meant to hold a fixture's weight. There's the immediate danger of falling glass fixtures, as well as the risk that the wires could be damaged, creating an electrical short and a fire hazard later. A ceiling fan is impossible to apply wallcovering around, so take it down.

Remove switchplates and outlet plates and protect the switches and outlets themselves with duct tape or blue painter's tape to shield. Tape switches in the "off" position as an additional safeguard against electrical shock.

Place a worktable in another room, or outside if you will be using solvents for cleaning. You can make a table by laying a piece of plywood or a flush wooden door over two sawhorses.

Place a large, lined trash can in the room to throw away debris as you work. Cleanup is not what you do at the end of the job, it's what you do throughout your project. A messy workplace is unsafe and can slow you down.

Bag the Hardware

I used to lay switchplates on the floor, then I would lose them under the drop cloth until I heard "crunch!" Then my wife came up with a brilliant solution using resealable storage bags. As you prepare the room, drop the switchplates into one medium-size plastic bag.

Remount screws back into their fixtures so they don't get lost or scratch the plastic plates. Separate the hardware for each window, door, and curtain into its own bag and mark its location in the room. Once all the hardware has been bagged and tagged, place the bags into one large bag with the room name on it. For safekeeping use blue painter's tape to stick the bag on the windowpane in the room.

My Mistake!

Whoops!

WHAT GOES UP CAN COME DOWN—FAST!

Whenever I get a new platform ladder, I always apply self-stick traction strips to the steps so I don't slip and fall. Aluminum is slippery enough—add a layer of water on top of it, and it can be like ice.

Well, I learned the hard way that you need to remove the old traction strips and apply new ones when the strip's adhesive starts to fail or the rough surface starts to wear. I was climbing my trusty platform ladder for the half-millionth time since I'd bought it, carrying a strip of wallcovering in both hands. Naturally, some of the water and wallcovering adhesive dripped onto the ladder step—right in the middle of where the traction strip had worn nearly through. I slipped, my feet went out from under me in a flash, and even though I was just on the first rung, barely a foot off the floor, my chin hit the top of the ladder on the way down and I knocked myself out.

I woke up 10 minutes later with a huge gash on my chin and blood all over the floor. Fortunately, I was on linoleum so I didn't ruin somebody's carpet. But the scar remains to remind me to this day.

Lesson learned:

Check your safety equipment periodically to make sure it still works. This goes not only for worn traction strips or cane tips on ladders, but worn, cracked, or slit insulation on extension cords, heat guards on work lights, lenses on goggles (if they're dirty you're less likely to wear them), and cartridges on respirators.

Strip It!
(Wallcovering, That Is!)

At every home show someone asks me how to remove wallcovering. It's the No. 1 technique people want to learn. It's a simple job—reverse hanging, actually. Ideally the paper should pull off the wall in fully intact sheets rather than the 4-inch strips created by a wallcovering scraper. Sound like magic? A bit of wizardry will help you remove wallcovering with ease.

The trick to removing an old wallcovering is to use tools and techniques that won't damage the surface or shred the wallcovering while dissolving the adhesive that bonds the wallcovering to the wall. Wallcovering adhesives are based on simple starch binders. For easy removal mix a special solution (page 71) that will attack the starch bonds between the wall and the covering.

THE SOLUTION

In my Secret Stripping Solution, water carries enzymes (the remover) that eat starch. Liquid fabric softener is a surfactant that makes the water wetter. When you add vinegar (a mild acid) and baking soda (a base) together, they create a carbonic gas reaction that turbocharges the solution. Placing a plastic sheet over the wall forces saturated solution through the holes made by the Paper Tiger. The solution is trapped under a sealed, nonporous plastic sheet that prevents it from drying, so the water-base solution can slowly break down the starch bonds that hold the wallcovering to the surface. TSP is an alkaline salt with a low pH value that needs to be neutralized by a mild acid-rinsing agent, such as white vinegar.

OTHER REMOVAL METHODS

Gel remover clings to the paper. It is especially effective for removing borders. Perforate the surface in the same manner as for wet removal, then apply the gel. Give it time to work properly in dissolving the wallcovering adhesive. Clean and rinse.

Steam removal is more dangerous than other methods, and it can damage the drywall behind the paper. If you do use a steam remover, perforate the surface in the same manner as for wet removal, then follow the manufacturer's instructions.

Wallcovering over wallcovering

Thinking about installing new wallcovering right over the old? Think again! Sure, you avoid the mess of removing the wallcovering, but the resulting finish is not as good. The old wallcovering's patterns and seam lines often show through the new material. Applying wallcovering paste to old paper can soften it and weaken its bond to the wall, potentially causing your new wallcovering to peel off. And it can be tough to clean dirt, grease, and other nasty stuff from old, porous wallcovering, which can prevent the new wallcovering from bonding well.

DRY REMOVAL

Fabric-backed vinyl or strippable solid-surface vinyl can often be removed using a dry stripping method.

1. Begin by peeling the top edge of a sheet of vinyl wallcovering away from the wall about 2 inches. Hold a dowel or broom handle against the wall and roll the paper around it in spool fashion.

2. Continue rolling the dowel down the wall, removing and rolling the paper as you work. The dowel keeps the pressure spread evenly across the sheet of paper, which can help prevent tearing. When you reach the bottom of the wall, slide the vinyl off the dowel and discard it. Start removing the next strip with a bare dowel. There are two types of vinyl wallcovering: solid vinyl or vinyl with a paper backing. If you're working with the latter, the vinyl will come off on your dowel roller, leaving the paper behind. Strip the paper backing with the wet-strip method after the vinyl is removed.

Secret Stripping Solution:

3 gallons hot water

22 ounces wallcovering remover concentrate with enzymes

¼ cup liquid fabric softener

1 cup white vinegar

2 tablespoons baking soda

WET REMOVAL

Use this method to remove more than one layer of wallcovering at a time. (I've removed more than a dozen layers at once this way.)

2

1. Turn off power to the room and remove the electrical cover plates. Place a strip of waterproof duct tape over the exposed electrical plugs and switches to shield them from water. You're going to be using a lot of water in this process, so cover the floors with plastic sheeting and an absorbent drop cloth or old towels. Secure the plastic sheeting along the edge of moldings with duct tape. The goal is to create a waterproof catch basin to avoid damaging the flooring. Change the absorbent drop cloth or towels frequently to ensure your floor stays dry.

2. Perforate the wallcovering with a Paper Tiger. The rotary teeth penetrate the surface of the wallcovering, allowing the solution to soak through and soften the adhesive. Use two Paper Tigers—one in each hand—to save time. Start at the top left corner of the wall and work down and across the wall, making large circles. Poke about 10 holes per square inch—enough to perforate, but not shred, the paper.

3

4

3. Pour the mixture into a clean garden sprayer, pressurize it, and adjust the nozzle for a medium mist. Spray the walls from the bottom up, working around the room in one direction. Apply the solution at least three times around the room. Mix a fresh batch as needed. To ensure that the chemical reaction is working effectively, move quickly; the solution remains active for only about 15 minutes.

4. When the walls are thoroughly saturated, smooth .7-mil plastic sheeting over the entire surface with a wallcovering brush and cut the plastic around the moldings to create a vacuum-tight seal. The secret is to trap the solution under the plastic. Leave the plastic on at least three hours—overnight is better—allowing the solution to dissolve the adhesive.

5. To test whether the adhesive has released, pull back a lower corner of the plastic and gently scrape the wallcovering from a corner with a paper scraper to see if it is loose enough for removal. If the wallcovering resists carefully lift the plastic about 6 inches away at the top of the wall in small areas and spray more solution to resoak the wallcovering. Then smooth the plastic back and let the solution work for an additional 6 to 12 hours. Allow the process to dissolve the adhesive by keeping it wet and you'll be rewarded by wallcovering that's very easy to remove.

6. When the adhesive has softened enough to remove the paper, fold about 4 feet of the plastic back toward a corner of the wall. Stick pushpins in the folded plastic so it doesn't fall down. Strip only one section at a time. Starting at the top of the wallcovering, lift the edge and begin scraping the wet paper backing off the wall. Position the scraping tool at a low attack angle to reduce surface gouging and damage. Spray on more removal solution to keep the paper moist; work from the top down, left to right. When that section is completely removed, fold back the next section of plastic and remove the wallcovering as described in the previous steps. Discard the stripped wallcovering into a garbage can with a plastic trash bag to keep the slippery, gooey mess off the floor.

Try the Iodine Test

Old adhesive left on the wall can prevent new wallcovering from sticking successfully. The iodine test shows if you have removed all adhesive. Mix 1 ounce of iodine with 1 quart of water and pour into a trigger-spray bottle. Spray the area where the wallcovering has been removed. If the iodine turns bluish purple, continue cleaning. Test again until you don't see any color on the wall. Spray the solution sparingly as iodine can stain if overused.

Lead and Asbestos

Lead and asbestos can be poisonous. Any home built before 1970 probably has materials in it that contain asbestos, and paint applied as recently as 1978 could contain lead. You may need to call a professional contractor to stabilize or remove those materials.

LEAD

The older the paint the more likely it contains lead. Years ago almost all paint included lead. With the development of latex paints, the use of lead-content paints declined from the 1950s until lead limits were set for all paints in 1978. Dust and chips from damaged or degraded lead paint can contaminate your house and cause serious health problems for you and your family. For safety any lead-bearing paint in your home that's loose, chipped, or breaking down should be professionally abated.

ASBESTOS

Asbestos has been linked to a number of serious lung diseases. Any home built before 1970 probably contains building materials made with asbestos—anything from sheet flooring to ceiling texture. If these materials are in good condition, they are generally not a threat. The problem with asbestos occurs when the fibers are disturbed and released into the air.

You can cover an asbestos-containing surface, such as a textured ceiling, with new wallboard or skim-coat it with wallboard compound. Don't try to scrape the texture off. If you want to remove it—or any material containing asbestos—hire an asbestos abatement contractor to take it off and dispose of it safely.

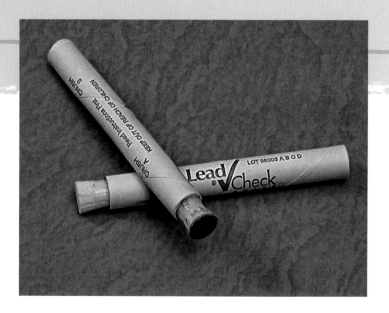

Test sticks, available at home centers and paint stores, reveal the presence of lead in paint. The tip turns red when rubbed over paint that contains lead. Follow the manufacturer's instructions.

Repairing Drywall Imperfections

I've seen this happen in both old and new houses: As the drywall settles it develops noticeable cracks, especially at stress points. Age can also open joints and expose popped nails. Don't let these routine repairs stress you out. I've developed easy methods to fix drywall problems once and for all.

REPAIRING POPPED NAILS

1. Drive a 1¼-inch wallboard screw into the stud or joist, about 2 inches from the popped nail so the head is slightly recessed. The screw should pull the wallboard tight against the framing.

2. Drive the popped nail down into the drywall.

3. With a 6-inch broad knife, cover the nail hole and screw head with lightweight surfacing compound. Let dry overnight; lightly wet-sand. Apply a thin second coat. Let it dry overnight.

4. Apply two coats of white-pigmented sealer to seal off the porous surfacing compound. This also keeps the paint sheen consistent, promotes proper adhesion for paint, and keeps color variations from showing through the paint.

1

2

3

4

CRACK ATTACK

Stress-point cracks are hard to repair permanently because they can reappear when the house shifts. The secret to filling such cracks is to use an interior vinyl spackling paste, which remains flexible, so it expands and contracts with the house.

1. If the crack is more than a hairline fissure but narrower than ¼ inch, widen it slightly and undercut its sides with a 10-in-1 tool. Vacuum, sponge, or brush out the crack to remove all the gypsum powder and paper.

2. With a 6-inch broad knife, apply interior vinyl surfacing compound using an overlapping technique and let dry. Sand with 120-grit sandpaper or wet-sand.

3. Reinforce the patched joint along its entire length with self-adhesive fiberglass-mesh or moistened paper joint tape. Apply more of the surfacing compound over the tape and let dry. If necessary sand again and apply a third coat with a wider knife.

4. Sand the patch and allow to dry.

5. Seal the repair with two coats of white-pigmented sealer.

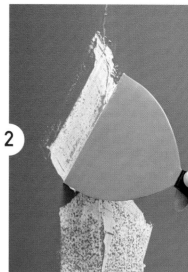
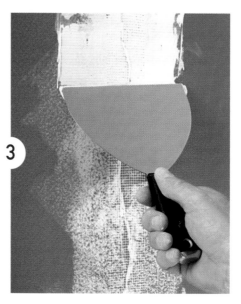

Got Paneling?

Never apply wallcovering directly over paneling. The irregularity of the paneled surface will show through. Either cover the paneling with a special liner paper, called "blank stock," or install ½-inch drywall over the paneling. Then install the wallcovering over the liner paper or the taped, mudded, and sealed drywall. For more information on installing drywall, see page 83.

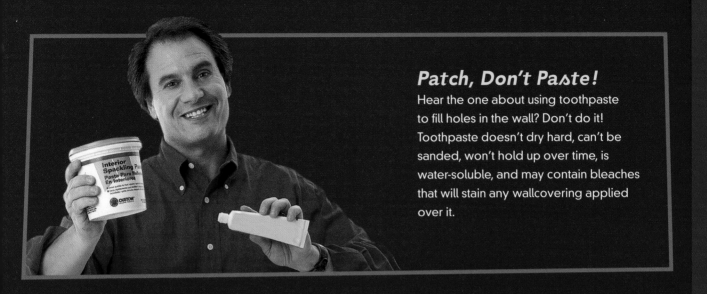

Patch, Don't Paste!

Hear the one about using toothpaste to fill holes in the wall? Don't do it! Toothpaste doesn't dry hard, can't be sanded, won't hold up over time, is water-soluble, and may contain bleaches that will stain any wallcovering applied over it.

Patching Small Holes

1. Spackle small holes in drywall or plaster by pressing the filler into the hole with a putty knife. Don't overfill. Two thin coats are better than one thick one.

2. To patch holes 1 to 4 inches across, such as a doorknob ding, put fiberglass-mesh reinforcing tape over the hole, then apply two coats of surfacing compound over the patch, letting it dry between coats. Sand lightly between coats.

3. To make quick work of sealing small repairs, use an aerosol can of quick-drying sealer, applied with a trigger sprayer. The spray can means quick coverage with no cleanup; the trigger makes it easy to apply.

1

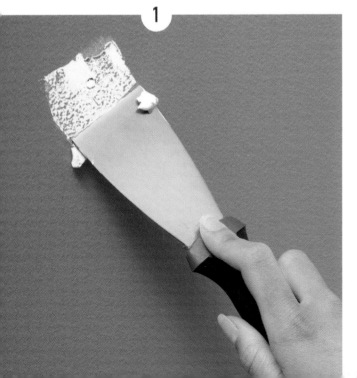

2

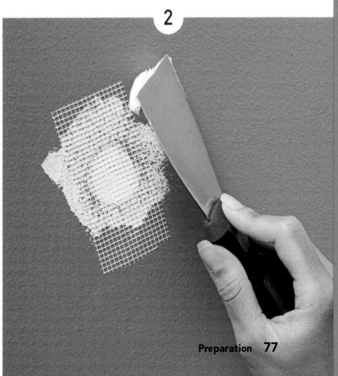

Repairing Large Holes

Need to repair a large hole, such as the one made when a doorknob gets pushed right through a wall? You deserve a wave of the Wizard's wand just for tackling the project! Large holes require a bit more patience and care to fix. Follow these directions, though, and you'll do fine.

1. Measure the hole. Cut a piece of drywall large enough to cover it. Trace around the patch onto the wall and, with a drywall saw, cut out the marked area. If the patch is large enough to extend from one stud to another, cut the opening to the center of each stud so you'll have nailing surfaces for the patch.

2. Cut one or more backer strips out of 1×2 boards, plywood, or drywall scraps. Make them 3 to 4 inches longer than the hole.

Sanding

Sanding is the key to a flawless wallcovering job, especially if you've done any wall patching or other repairs. In most situations light dry-sanding will be enough to remove peaks of patching material and polish the surface. A wallboard sanding screen, handheld sanding block, or power sander works well for large jobs. Don't use a belt sander; it will abrade the surface too much.

Sand drywall and plaster along the longest direction. Wear a respirator and seal off the room to keep dust from spreading. Place a box fan in the window so it will suck fine dust out of the room and exhaust it outside. This works best if you open another window or door—ideally on a wall opposite the fan—to ensure cross-ventilation and a good supply of clean air.

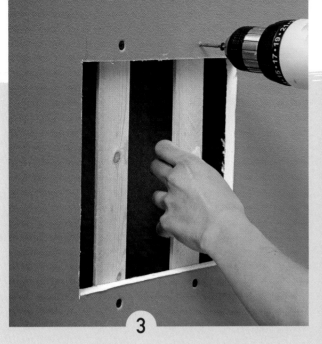

3

3. Slip the backer strips behind the opening and secure them to the wall with 1-inch wallboard screws. Lightly coat the edges of the hole and the patch with joint compound. Push the patch into the opening and fasten it to the backer strips with drywall screws. If the ends lay on studs, fasten the patch to the studs as well.

4. Apply strips of self-adhesive fiberglass-mesh tape or moistened paper joint tape to the seams, overlapping the tape at the corners of the patch. Work a coat of joint compound into and over the tape, making horizontal and vertical sweeps. This is called the *crisscross technique.* Let dry overnight. Sand with 120-grit sandpaper. Skim a second coat of compound over the entire patch. Let the patch dry completely.

5. Sand with 120-grit sandpaper and seal with white-pigmented oil-base sealer.

5

Patching on White

When patching white walls or molding, mix two drops of red food coloring into every 6 ounces of surfacing compound to make it easy to spot repairs.

My Mistake!

When in a hurry, slow down

I was hanging wallcovering in a bathroom many years ago. There was a big dent in the drywall where someone had thrown the door open too hard one too many times and the knob had mashed into the wall.

I was young and in a hurry, so I used some so-called hot mud—drywall compound that's formulated to set up quickly so you don't have to wait overnight for it to dry.

Set up quickly it did. As soon as it felt firm to the touch, I papered right over it with a nice, shiny vinyl-coated paper with a foil finish to it. At first it looked great—no more dent, great-looking wallcovering. But when I came back into the room the next day after working elsewhere in the house, I discovered an ugly surprise. Not only had the dent partially reappeared, but also the wallcovering had discolored where I'd applied the compound. I had to cut out the whole section, repair it the slow, old-fashioned way, and install a patch. Hardly timesaving.

 Lesson learned:
Follow the package directions when using surfacing or drywall compound. Put on several thin coats rather than trying to fill a big dent with one application. If you don't the surface of the patch will feel dry, but the material is still wet underneath. While drying, it can give off chemicals that stain the paper—and shrink in the process, making the smooth-as-glass repair magically disappear.

Repairing Plaster

If you have extensive damage to areas larger than 12 inches square, have a professional plasterer do the work. For smaller cracks and holes, do it yourself by cleaning out the crack with a 10-in-1 tool, then filling it with surfacing compound. Sand smooth.

REINFORCING LOOSE PLASTER

This repair sounds harder than it really is. When plaster is sound but sagging away from the underlying lath, you can repair it by screwing it to the lath.

1. Thread a plaster washer onto a 1½-inch wallboard screw. Drive the screw through the plaster into the lath using a power drill/driver. Drive the screw in until the washer is drawn into the plaster surface. Space the screws 4 inches apart and drive them into studs or joists whenever possible.

2. Cover the washers and the crack with vinyl surfacing compound. Let dry thoroughly.

3. Sand the area with 120-grit sandpaper or wet-sand. Sand the patches flush with the wall (or ceiling).

4. Seal the repaired area with white-pigmented shellac.

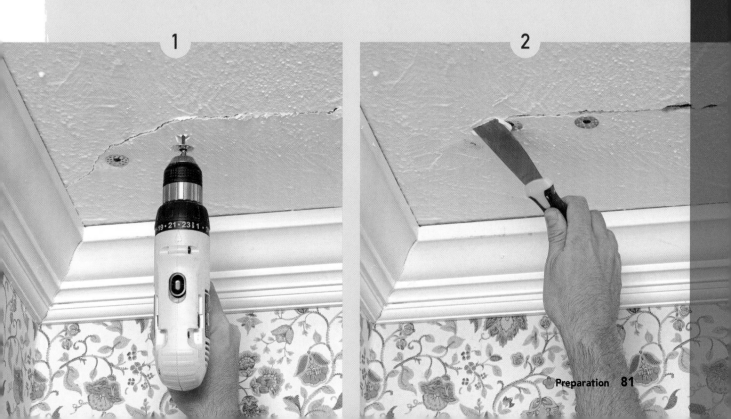

REPAIRING SMALL HOLES IN PLASTER

1. Remove loose material. Dust the area with a dusting brush or remove any loose debris with a shop vacuum. Dampen the edges of the plaster with a commercial latex bonding agent (or use my money-saving alternative mixture—see "Kitchen Aid," below); mix and apply it according to manufacturer's instructions. Then mix patching plaster according to manufacturer's instructions. Apply the plaster with a broad knife. If the hole is less than ¼ inch deep, one coat should be enough for good coverage. If the hole is deeper than ¼ inch, apply a base coat of plaster in the hole to within ¼ inch of the surface. Press the plaster into the lath. Let this coat set for 15 minutes.

2. Score the surface with a nail to provide tooth for the next layer. The resulting roughened texture will give the second coat something to grip. Let the base dry overnight.

3. Apply a second layer of patching plaster, bringing it almost to the surface. Let this layer set for at least an hour. Add water to bring the patching plaster to a creamy consistency for the finish coat. Apply the finish coat as smoothly as possible. Make the patched area flush with the surrounding surface. Let the finish coat set for at least an hour.

4. Smooth the patch with a damp sponge, blending it into the surrounding surface. This will reduce the amount of sanding necessary. Let the plaster harden. Seal the area with white-pigmented shellac.

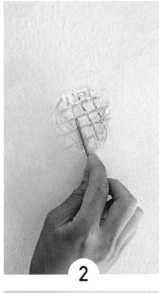

Kitchen Aid

Make an inexpensive bonding agent with common dishwashing liquid. To make the solution add a drop to a bucket of water and substitute for the commercial latex bonding agent used to repair holes in plaster.

Installing Drywall

If you apply wallcoverings directly over a textured surface, the texture telegraphs through the material, ruining the effect. So one of the questions I'm asked often in my wallcovering workshops is how to smooth a textured surface. My answer? Cover it up with new ¼- or ⅜-inch drywall. It's usually faster, easier, and cleaner than other choices. And it allows you to apply wallcoverings where once you could only paint.

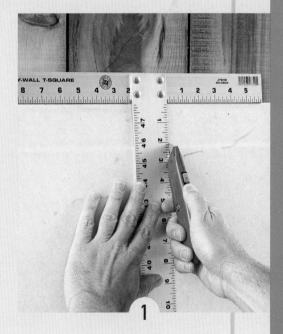

I can install and smooth a piece of drywall with two coats of mud in one day; trying to smooth paneling with many coats of mud takes longer. Drywall adds structural rigidity and sound-dampening qualities that give your home a more solid feel. Drywall sheets are 4 feet wide and commonly available in lengths of 8 or 10 feet (⅜-inch sheets can also be found in 12- or 14-foot sizes). Measure your wall and determine the sizes of the sheets and their arrangement on the wall (horizontal or vertical) to create the fewest seams and partial sheets possible. Don't place new seams directly over old seams.

Moisture-resistant drywall panels are good for use in kitchens or bathrooms. Secure the sheets in place with drywall screws or, better yet, use a combination of screws and construction adhesive. Doing so creates a more solid bond and also allows you to use fewer screws, speeding installation and mudding.

Remove all of the woodwork from the surface, both at the top and the bottom of the walls. Mark the location of the wall studs so you can easily find them as you install the new drywall sheets. Place a light pencil mark on the ceiling at the point of each stud. Mark the locations of electrical boxes.

1. Use a utility knife to cut through the outside face of drywall and into the gypsum. Guide the cut with a drywall T-square or a carpenter's square. Make two or three passes to deepen the cut; you don't have to cut all the way through.
To complete the cut, hold the sheet and bump the backside with your knee to snap the gypsum. Slice through the back with a knife.

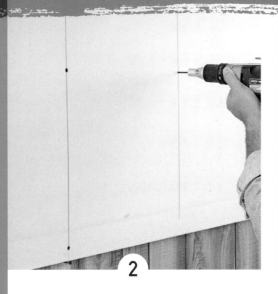

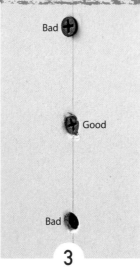

2

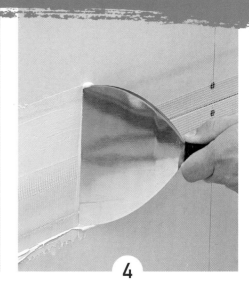

3

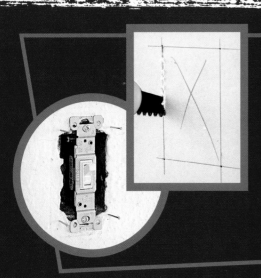

4

2. Just before you put up a sheet, run a heavy bead of caulk around the top and corners of the wall. This secures the edges of the drywall and fills any air pockets around the perimeter of the drywall sheet. With a helper lift each sheet into place. Handle the sheets carefully; they are heavy and awkward and can break. Drive screws or nails through the sheet into the wall studs. Begin in the center of a panel and work outward. Space nails or screws about 12 inches apart, 16–18 inches apart if you're using construction adhesive as well.

3. Set screwheads or nailheads just below the surface of the panel, creating a slight dimple, but do not break the paper facing. If a screw head does break through the paper, place another screw right next to it.

4. Fill screw or nail dimples with joint compound using a 6-inch drywall knife. Cover the joints with self-adhesive fiberglass-mesh tape, then cover the tape with a coat of drywall compound. Let the first coat dry 24 hours, scrape off ridges and globs, and apply a second coat with a 10-inch drywall knife. Let the second coat dry and apply a third coat, feathering out the edges of the compound. Smooth the surface by sponging or sanding. Sanding creates dust; wear a dust mask and eye protection.

Mark Studs and Outlets

Before installing drywall mark the location of studs with a light pencil mark on the ceiling. This lets you know where they are so you can drive the drywall screws firmly into the wall's structure. Mark electrical boxes by driving two 3-inch finishing nails into the studs near the top and bottom of the box. Allow the nailheads to protrude about 1 inch above the surface, then press the drywall sheet up against the wall and remove it. The protruding nailheads will indent the backside of the drywall, showing you where to make the cutouts for the electrical boxes.

Mudding Textured Walls

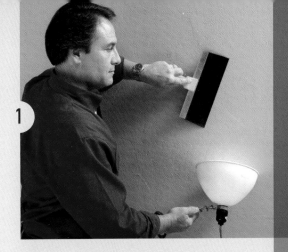

Sometimes it's impractical to install drywall over a textured surface: The room may be small and awkward to work in, for instance. Or delicate moldings, trimwork, or other built-in features may not allow you to add a sheet material to the surface without dramatically changing the character of the room.

Rather than sanding the texture from a wall, it is easier to fill in, or float, over the texture that exists. This technique is known as *mudding*.

1. Clear out the room and clean the walls.

2. Lightly sand the entire wall with a pole sander and a 120-grit sanding screen to knock down any roughness or high peaks on the wall. This drastically reduces the time and material you'll need to achieve a smooth surface. Do not scrape textured surfaces. Dust the walls with a clean broom or vacuum.

   If there are any damaged areas on the wall, spot-seal the areas by applying two coats of white-pigmented oil-base sealer to the wall. Use a disposable brush or a roller with a disposable cover. Let dry, which will take 45 minutes to 1 hour. Sand lightly with a 120-grit sanding screen.

3. Thin premix joint compound with water in a 5-gallon bucket until it is the consistency of a heavy meringue. Adding water makes the compound more liquid to improve the flow. Mix thoroughly to a uniform consistency using a drill equipped with a propeller-type drywall compound mixing tool. Don't use a mixer designed for paint—it won't adequately stir the compound, which is thicker than paint.

4. Before applying compound divide the wall into 4-foot-square sections. Scoop the compound into a stainless-steel or plastic drywall tray.

5

5. Sharpen the edge of your drywall knife by moving it back and forth briskly across the surface of your drywall sander. This removes any rust from the broad knife so it doesn't stain the mud, which can show through to the final finish. This polishing also removes any dings or imperfections in the edge of the blade.

6. Wash and rinse dirt and metal shavings off the blade using a clean tile sponge in a bucket of clean water. Do this after you've completed each 4×4 section of wall to prevent dried mud from building up on the blade and to keep the blade wet so the mud flows smoothly from blade to wall. When working with mud, wetter is better.

7. Apply mud to the wall with 4-foot-long horizontal strokes. This is called *laying on*. Strive for a relatively even coat but don't worry about creating a perfectly smooth finish at this stage.

8. Scrape off excess mud that may remain on your broad knife. Then stroke the mud vertically from top to bottom, working from left to right to create a crosshatch effect. This makes a thin, even coat without the ridges that can result from stroking in only one direction. As you're making the final stroke, angle the broad knife slightly in the direction you're moving it to avoid leaving ridges in the mud.

6

7

8

9

10

11

9. Feather the mud into corners by running the broad knife vertically down the wall with a nice, even stroke. Bring the broad knife as close to the adjacent wall surface as possible without actually touching it. This helps avoid ripples and ridges in the finish caused by texture on the adjacent wall.

10. Let the wall dry overnight, then scrape off any ridges by moving a sharp broad knife back and forth over the surface at a low angle. This process is called *kerfing*.

11. Wet-sand the surface using a green scouring pad and a bucket of clean water. Dip the pad in the water, then wring it until it is damp but not dripping. Move it in a gentle circular motion over the surface to knock down the high spots. This also fills low spots with a paste made of excess material removed from the high spots mixed with the moisture in the sponge. A sponge that's too wet will simply wash the material off the wall. Leave as much material on the wall as possible while smoothing the surface for the next application.

Wizards Work Wet

Wetter is better! The cleaner you keep your tools, the better your job will be. And in this case, clean means wet. If you keep your tools wet, mud won't dry on the tool, build up, and roughen the edge, which creates streaks in your finish. Working wet also prevents dried chunks of mud from flaking off the tool and embedding themselves in the finish, creating more streaks or divots as you move the tool over them. Those streaks or divots will require an additional coat of mud to correct, prolonging the job.

12. Clean as you go. Drywall mud is much easier to clean up when it's wet—you can just wipe up an errant dollop with a sponge. After it dries you have to chisel or sand it off.

13. Two thin coats are better than one thick one. After your wet-sanding job on the first coat has dried, apply a second coat. Note how the angle at which I'm holding the broad knife results in a ridge of excess material on one side of the knife only.

14. Let the second coat dry and wet-sand it as you did with the first coat. This time, use a slightly finer-grit white scouring pad. Lightly polish the surface; don't abrade it severely.

15. Use a dish scrubber filled with water to work into corners and around moldings. The hollow handle gives you reach and leverage and allows you to slightly dampen the scrubbing surface with water whenever it gets a bit too dry.

Wizards Work Clean

The bane of every home remodeling job is drywall dust. It's insidious stuff—very fine and very messy. It gets into everything—your carpets, your fabrics, your ductwork and furnace filters, everything. So one of the main goals in mudding is to create a smooth finish that minimizes the need for sanding afterwards Whenever you can, wet-sand rather than dry-sand. Wet-sanding goes a long way toward minimizing dust. And it creates a smoother finish with less work because the process actually adds drywall compound to low spots while removing it from high spots. And that means you typically can apply fewer coats of mud to get the same effect compared with dry-sanding, which only removes high spots.

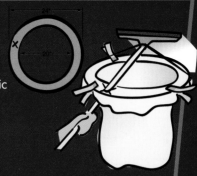
Removing Ceiling Texture

Now that you've smoothed the walls, why stop there? If your house was built in recent decades, chances are you have a textured "popcorn" ceiling. I hate the stuff! It traps dust, turning your ceiling gray or black around heating and air-conditioning vents, it's difficult to paint, and pieces crumble and fall off if you brush against it. That can result in crumbs of texture falling between your wallcoverings and the wall as you install wallcoverings, creating irregularities in the surface. I say get rid of it now, while the room is cleared out and your tools are at hand.

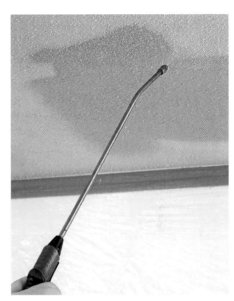

Remove any nonasbestos texturing by soaking it with a solution of 1 cup ammonia and 1 cup fabric softener added to 1 gallon of water. This procedure can make a big mess, so cover the floor well with taped-down plastic before you start. Apply the solution with a spray bottle or garden sprayer and let it soak in for about 15 minutes. Then scrape the softened texture off the ceiling with a floor squeegee.

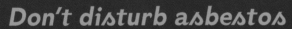

Don't disturb asbestos

A textured ceiling, especially one that was sprayed before 1970, could contain asbestos. For that reason alone do not attempt to remove the texture if you are not sure whether asbestos is present. Always assume texture material contains asbestos until a test proves otherwise. For more information see page 74.

Overlaying a Textured Ceiling

You can cover the ceiling with drywall the same way you would a wall. If you are installing more than a half-dozen ceiling panels, consider renting a wallboard jack. This device raises or lowers a full sheet of drywall with a simple crank. It has wheels so you can position the wallboard easily. With a jack one person can install ceiling panels.

To hang just a few wallboard sheets, use a T-support. While it's a bit more cumbersome to use than a wallboard jack, you can make one yourself for a couple of bucks and it will save you two trips to the rental store. Cut one 2×4 about 40 inches long. Cut another piece to a length equal to the distance from the floor to the ceiling of the room, minus 1 inch plus the thickness of the wallboard (1½ inches for ½-inch drywall). Fasten the long piece to the center of the short one at a right angle. Add braces for strength. Hold the support so the cross member of the T is near the ceiling, with the T's leg resting on the floor at an angle. With helpers position a sheet of drywall on the ceiling, then move the leg of the brace toward the vertical until the T's cross member holds the wallboard snug against the ceiling.

Before installation use a stud finder to locate the ceiling joists. Mark the location of each joist on the top of an adjacent wall with a light pencil mark so you'll know where to place fasteners when installing the ceiling panels. Install panels parallel to joists. If possible use panels long enough to span from wall to wall.

Lift the first panel into place and attach it through the existing ceiling surface and into the joists with 1¾-inch type W wallboard screws using a drill/driver. Begin in the center of the panel and work outward. Stagger any unavoidable end joints at least 16 inches. If you cut any panels full length, place the cut edge against the wall and leave a slight gap. Place screws no closer than ⅜ inch to panel edges. Set screw heads just below the surface of the panel but do not break through the paper facing. If a screw head does break through the paper, place another screw right next to it. Embed screwheads far enough into the paper for joint compound to cover them. Tape and finish the drywall joints.

Cleaning Up

Cleaning a surface before applying wallcovering is just as important as any of the other steps. That's because wallcoverings are films: Anything on the wall that's biologically or chemically active will come through eventually and ruin your job.

Mildew, oil, and grease will prevent adhesives from bonding to the wall. Rust and water stains will show through the new covering. Even the most expensive wallcoverings are only as good as the surface to which you apply them.

Here's another point worth repeating: An empty room is an easy room to work in. When everything has been removed, clean the floor and baseboards. Cover the floor with plastic sheeting, securing the edges to the floor with duct tape. Then add a layer of drop cloths to protect from splatters of wallcovering stripper and wallcovering adhesive. Cover any remaining furnishings with .7-mil plastic sheeting.

CLEANING THE WALLS

Clean walls are essential for helping wallcoverings adhere. After washing a wall allow it to dry for a day before you apply wallcovering. This job is much easier when one person scrubs and another rinses.

First dust off all surfaces with a vacuum cleaner or sweep with a clean dust mop. Set up two separate 5-gallon buckets with two sponge-head mops, one for washing the surfaces, the other for rinsing off the dirt. Mark the handle of the mop used for washing with red duct tape to prevent mixing up mops. Fill your cleaning bucket with 3 gallons of warm water and add ¾ cup TSP (trisodium phosphate). Mix well. Using a sponge mop with a scrubbing head, wash the wall in 8-foot widths, from the bottom up, working around the room (photo below left). When you reach your starting point, turn the mop head around and begin scrubbing the wall with the nylon scrubbing head (photo below right).

No matter what you're washing, change the cleaning solution often to prevent putting dirt and grease back onto the surface. After scrubbing the first 8-foot section, use the rinsing solution immediately to remove the dirt and the cleaner off the surfaces. Fill your rinsing bucket with 3 gallons of warm water and add 3 cups of distilled white vinegar. Mix well. Using the rinse solution, wipe down with the second mop. Change this solution often. The vinegar acts as an astringent and neutralizes the phosphors that could prevent the wallcovering adhesive from bonding properly to a surface.

Washing

Scrubbing

Tackling Tough Stains

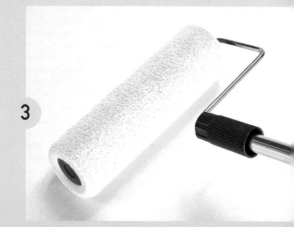

MOLD AND MILDEW

Regardless of where you live, you may be plagued with mold and mildew. Look for splotches on your walls. If you find some dab them with a small amount of household bleach. If the spot comes off, it's not dirt—it is mold or mildew.

1. To remove mold and mildew, mix 1 cup household cleaner and 2 cups of hydrogen peroxide in 1 gallon warm water. Wear gloves and goggles. Apply the solution with a sponge or mop and let stand for several minutes. Several applications may be needed. Rinse with a solution of 1 cup vinegar in a gallon of water.

2. When dry, lightly sand the places where the mildew appeared.

3. Seal against another outbreak by applying two coats of white-pigmented oil-base sealer. Sand lightly between coats.

GREASE STAINS

Stubborn grease stains require an additional cleaning step. To remove, rub them with a liquid deglosser to break the oil film. When dry, sand with 120-grit paper, then wipe away the sanding dust. Seal with two coats of white-pigmented oil-base sealer. Sand lightly between coats.

RUST AND WATER STAINS

Rust and water stains will show through paint. To remove these spots scrub with a solution of ¼ cup Epsom salts in 1 cup warm water. Rinse with a mixture of 1 cup vinegar in a gallon of warm water. Allow to dry for several days, then sand with 120-grit sandpaper. Seal with two coats of white-pigmented oil-base sealer. Sand lightly between coats.

Grime Time

Think your walls are grime-free? Try this test: Spray a tissue with water and lightly rub it on the wall. See that brown smudge? It's body oils, hair spray, and food oils that become airborne while cooking and eventually settle on the walls. Many wallcovering jobs fail because wallcoverings are applied on top of dingy, dirty surfaces. Clean before you cover.

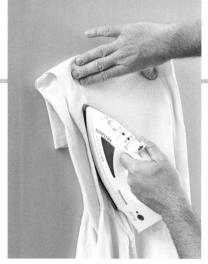

MARKER AND CRAYON STAINS

With three children, I've tackled more than my share of crayon marks on the wall. The best way to remove these stains is to fold an old T-shirt into a pad several layers thick and place it over a crayon mark, then run an iron set at medium heat over the pad (above left and center). If it doesn't remove the mark entirely, heat the mark with a hair dryer and blot away as much of the mark as possible (above right). Seal with two coats of white-pigmented oil-base sealer, sanding lightly between coats.

For scribbles from permanent markers, lightly dab the spot with nail polish remover. Rub the spot with a liquid deglosser. When dry, sand with 120-grit paper, then wipe away the sanding dust. Seal with two coats of white-pigmented oil-base sealer. Sand between coats.

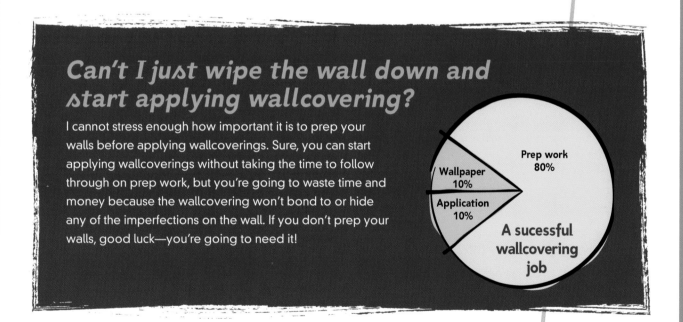

Can't I just wipe the wall down and start applying wallcovering?

I cannot stress enough how important it is to prep your walls before applying wallcoverings. Sure, you can start applying wallcoverings without taking the time to follow through on prep work, but you're going to waste time and money because the wallcovering won't bond to or hide any of the imperfections on the wall. If you don't prep your walls, good luck—you're going to need it!

Wallpaper 10%
Application 10%
Prep work 80%

A sucessful wallcovering job

Cleaning Ceilings

Smooth, previously painted ceilings can be cleaned this way: Mix 1 cup of vinegar and 2 tablespoons of baking soda in 1 gallon water and spray the solution on with a garden sprayer. Mop and rinse the same way you would if cleaning a wall.

Caulk Is King

The secret to perfectly trimmed wallpaper is not in the cutting—it's in the caulking. Before I apply wallcovering to any room, I always caulk the entire room along baseboards and around window and door trim with a white water-base acrylic caulk. I even caulk inside corners.

There are several reasons to do this. First it can help make your home more energy efficient if any air is leaking through the cracks. Second the caulk eliminates gaps, giving the room a more finished look. Finally—and this is why I caulk even where there are no gaps or air leakages—the caulk makes it much easier to make a clean cut when trimming the wallcovering after application. Acrylic latex caulk especially lends resilience to the surface, allowing your trimming knife's blade to glide along easily and stay sharp longer than if you were trying to cut against wood, plaster, or drywall. The result is a neat, precise, almost effortless cut that more than repays the few minutes it takes to apply the caulk. When you open the caulk tube, cut the tip at an angle at the mark for a small bead (photo above right).

Don't Be a Drip!

Caulking is a pretty easy task, and it makes a huge difference when you trim your wallcovering. But it's also a job that typically involves some drips—of caulk, that is. The problem is that most caulking guns don't know when to stop pushing caulk out of the tube, so when you reach the end of a seam, the caulk just keeps coming, leaving a big blob in the corner or dripping all over the floor. Save yourself some cleanup by buying a dripless caulking gun: As soon as you release pressure on the trigger, the caulk stops—right where you want it to.

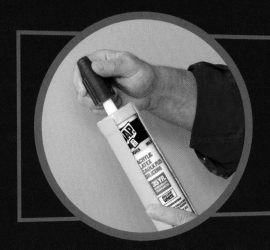

Cap It!

To prevent unused caulk from drying out in the tube and plugging the tip, screw a large wire nut, available at hardware stores and home centers, on the tip.

Caulking is one of the easiest, most satisfying pieces of prep work you'll do. The trick is to squeeze the caulking gun's trigger evenly while moving the tip of the caulk tube smoothly and at a constant speed. Pull the gun toward the uncaulked part of the seam, leaving a smooth bead of caulking material trailing from the tip of the tube (above left and opposite page). Don't stop to smooth the bead while you're laying down caulk—keep going until you reach the end of the seam. Then go back over the seam with a damp sponge, if neccessary, to remove any globs or wobbles (above right). Keep a bucket of water handy and rinse the sponge continually to prevent caulk from building up on the sponge and smearing onto the wall. Allow to dry overnight.

Seal the Deal: All About Sealers and Primers

Sealers seal, primers prepare surfaces, and sizers restrict porosity. It's not enough to clean walls before you apply wallcovering over them. You also have to seal surfaces that have never been painted. Sealers and primers also provide tooth, a slightly roughened surface to which wallcovering adhesives can bond.

SEALERS

Sealer, also called undercoater, is a prep coat that forms a barrier against moisture and isolates problem areas such as those plagued by mold, stains, or discoloration. Sealers are also used on brand-new walls in baths, kitchens, and other high-moisture areas to help wallcoverings bond well, yet allow them to be easily stripped off later if desired. Sealer products include white-pigmented shellacs and oil-base undercoats. Apply a sealer in two thin coats, sanding lightly—and I do mean lightly—between coats with 220-grit sandpaper. You want to scratch the surface just enough to allow for a good bond. If you're creating a lot of dust, you're sanding way too much.

PRIMERS

Clear primers are used to cover painted walls before applying wallcovering. These products bond to even glossy paint surfaces while giving the wallcovering adhesive a good bonding surface. They're generally acrylic, water-base products, so they're a bit easier to use than sealers and tend to dry faster.

SIZERS

Sizers are used less frequently these days because they're designed for use on plaster and most walls nowadays are drywall. A sizer is actually a dilution of wallpaper adhesive that's designed to temper the porosity of a plaster wall. Raw plaster is so porous that it can literally absorb all the wallcovering adhesive, leaving nothing on the surface of the wall to hold the wallcovering on. If you've patched a plaster wall, use a sizer on the patched area to assure good adhesion.

TV vs. reality

"Those reality decorating shows never show people washing walls," you say. "Why should I?" Good question. But do not take lessons in process from what you see on entertainment television. As a wallcovering contractor, I'd be quickly out of business if I did things the way you see them done on those reality decorating shows: no prepping the room, no cleaning the walls, people doing five things to a room at a time—trust me, these shows are entertainment, not instruction. There's simply no substitute for following the steps. Rush things, and the result is a mess. Skipping past preparation may make a TV show better, but not your living room walls.

Working With a Professional Wallcovering Contractor

Sometimes the job you have in mind is too big, complicated, or time-consuming to do it yourself. Perhaps after reading this book, you'll decide that you'd like to hire someone to do all or some of the wallcovering installation you want. I always encourage people to try it themselves. But we all have demands on our time and attention, and there's nothing wrong with calling in a pro. If you do, take the responsibility to check out any installer you're thinking of hiring thoroughly before contracting the job.

WHEN CHOOSING A WALLCOVERING INSTALLER:

☆ Always get a written estimate for every job, along with a price list detailing how costs for any additional work will be calculated. Those estimates make sure that both you and the contractor agree on exactly what work will be done and on what date it will start. The law in many states requires contractors to provide customers with a written estimate, as it gives consumers recourse in any legal disputes that may arise. If you agree to the job, both you and the contractor should have a copy of the estimate that is signed and dated by both parties. The price list lets you know in advance how much any additional work will cost, should it be required.

☆ Never tell a contractor the price of other estimates you've received. That assures that you get an unbiased bid and the best deal in the end.

☆ Expect a professional job, no matter the cost. If you wanted it done halfway, you wouldn't hire a pro.

☆ Professionals should be on time. There is absolutely no excuse for someone not showing up when they say they will or at least calling if they will be a few minutes late.

☆ When a contractor arrives to give an estimate, ask to see a contractor's license or a driver's license. I can't tell you how many people have opened their doors and allowed me to walk right into their homes without asking for proof that I was who I said I was.

☆ Be safe. The first time you arrange to meet any stranger in your home, have a friend, neighbor, or family member with you or carry a cordless or cell phone. Before giving work crews access to your home, ask for a photocopy of each crew member's driver's license so you have positive identification of who they are and how to reach them.

☆ Look for someone who treats their work like a business. Dress, demeanor, even the condition of their vehicle should be neat and professional, and they should be interested in listening to you and working with you to provide the results you want.

☆ Respect the contractor's knowledge but don't let it intimidate you. Ask lots of questions and, if you can't get something explained to your satisfaction, choose another contractor.

☆ Ask to see a portfolio of the contractor's work and for references of previous customers, with phone numbers. If possible visit these customers in person to look at the job. Ask the customer if he or she was satisfied with the work, if the results were as agreed upon, if communication was good throughout the job, and if the contractor was neat, careful, and on time.

Get everything in writing. Once you've chosen an installer, you need to agree to a contract that covers all aspects of the job:

☆ Determine who is responsible for doing the prep work. If the contractor will do the prep work, have that work spelled out in the contract. If you're responsible for the prep work, understand clearly what's expected of you. I always mark up any walls I'm going to work on in a client's house with two colors of chalk: one to show areas that need to be sanded, another to show areas that need to be filled. If you're going to do the prep, have the contractor sign off on your job once you've finished it, agreeing that you performed the work properly.

☆ Understand what condition the walls, room, and workspace are to be in upon the contractor's arrival. I hand clients a sheet detailing the condition I expect the workspace to be in upon my arrival, along with a price sheet detailing how much I'll charge if I have to, for example, clean a bathroom or remove furniture from a living room.

☆ Agree on a payment method. Most contractors charge a stated fee per single roll of wallcovering installed. That fee can range from $10 to $40 per single roll and varies widely depending on the material, the job, the region, and the contractor. Be aware that the number of rolls of wallcovering used to cover a given room will also vary with the type of material and the pattern. A large drop match pattern may create 22 percent waste, and a uniform material such as grass cloth may have as little as 1 percent waste. Because more material results in more handling and more time involved in cutting, trimming, and pattern matching, the per-roll charge is a fair and widely used method of accounting for these differences.

☆ Before you agree on an installation price, find out if that price includes preparation. Often it does not: Prep is charged based on a per-square-foot fee. Square footage is calculated as the actual square footage of the room minus the space taken up by doors and windows. That's also a fair way to charge, as the contractor has to touch that amount of wall in order to prepare it correctly. Contractors may charge a single fee for any preparation involved, or they may have a price list that breaks out square-foot costs for various operations such as stripping, mudding, and priming. Keep in mind, too, that difficulty gets factored in: If you have a two-story stairwell that will require the use of scaffolding or a really chopped-up bathroom that's going to require lots of trimming and cutting, you can expect to pay more than for a similar-size, 8-foot-tall blank wall.

☆ Understand change orders. It's not unusual for a contractor to start a job and discover the unexpected—deteriorated plaster, for example, hidden by a previous wallcovering. In that case the contractor should write a detailed change order listing the additional work required and calculating an additional fee to compensate for that work, using the same rates as were used to calculate the original job. You and the contractor then sign and date the change order, and it is appended to the original contract. That keeps you informed of the negotiated price, and it holds the contractor accountable to the project as it has evolved.

Chapter 4

Application

Here's where the covering hits the wall! Thanks to all the preparation you've done, you'll probably be able to wallpaper a standard-size room in one day or less by following the techniques described here. It's natural to be excited—nothing can transform a room better, faster, or more thoroughly than wallcoverings. But don't rush. Follow the steps, and I'll be looking over your shoulder to guide you through the process.

If you have never installed wallpaper, start with a simple room—one with flat walls and few doors and windows—or a room where errors may not matter as much. A child's room or laundry room is a better place for your first wallpapering project than the more public living room or kitchen. With a little practice you can tackle more prominent rooms with confidence.

When it comes to installing wallcoverings, two people can do the job far better than one. Working together—one person cutting and prepping the paper and the other person putting it on the wall—makes wallpapering easy.

Many people who install wallcoverings—including many professionals—simply start pasting up sheets of paper in a corner, cutting, pasting, installing, and trimming the sheets as they go. That's a terrible way to work! You're constantly going back and forth from one operation to another and one set of tools to another. Your tape measure gets all gooey from paste, you can't find your trimming knife, the paper you just pasted is drying out while you look for your framing square, and the whole operation is much more complex, frustrating, and time-consuming than it need be. This chapter shows a better way to do it.

The Henry Ford Method

I'm going to introduce you to a better way to install wallcovering. I call it the Henry Ford method of installing wallcoverings. Henry Ford created a production line that could build 43 cars in the time his competitors could build one. I'll show you how to do the same thing when installing wallcoverings. Rather than trying to do several operations at once, you'll plan the job first, prepare the wallcovering for installation second, and install it third. Wizards plan ahead, then act with confidence.

I'll break each operation down into easy-to-follow steps that group like tasks. You'll do all the cutting at once, all the trimming at once, and all the installing at once. The result: You'll be able to complete your job in one-third the time or less. And once you've gotten the hang of the work (so to speak), it's a lot less stressful and chaotic than installing wallcovering sheet by sheet, and it results in a much higher quality, more professional-looking job.

It all starts with a well-planned layout that shows where each sheet will go on the walls. Here's an essential point: Layout and installation are two entirely different processes.

• Layout is foreseeing what the installation will look like: where each sheet will go, where each seam will fall, how the wallcovering's pattern, if there is one, will be placed on the wall.

• Installation is the process of installing the wallpaper in the room in accordance with the layout you've planned.

If you start applying wallcoverings before you've settled on a layout, you almost certainly will end up with awkward seam locations, strips of wallcovering too narrow for proper adhesion, pattern mismatches in conspicuous places, or a strong wallcovering pattern that feels out of balance with the room's focal point. To avoid such problems follow the four planning principles explained on the opposite page: They are not laws; they're guidelines.

Process Vs. Product

The product reflects the process. If you have the process down, the result looks great. So bear with me for a moment while we go over how we get the job done right. I'm about to show you a great bag of wizard tricks that may seem complex now, but they'll ultimately make the process go much more smoothly. The ultimate result: fantastic walls!

1. Create a trial layout that starts at the vertical centerline of the room's focal point wall (I'll talk more about how to identify this wall on pages 106–107). From this starting point the layout will show you where seams will fall across this wall and around the room.

2. Put the last seam, which usually mismatches, in a dead corner—the most inconspicuous spot in the room. Common dead corners include behind doors, the header space above the entrance, and hidden alcoves.

3. Reduce the number of full-length seams by planning or adjusting the layout to place some seams within windows and doors.

4. Try to leave half a sheet—or at the very least a strip no narrower than 6 inches—beside a door or window.

The overall goal is to minimize the seams and maximize the width of each sheet.

Remember, these guidelines are not absolute. Sometimes you'll need to make compromises based on the room's dimensions, the wallcovering pattern repeat, the location of doors, windows, moldings, and corners, and other factors that won't become apparent until you've finished your layout. The first trial layout you develop may not satisfy all of these principles. Consider it a first draft and keep applying the principles, making adjustments and compromises, until you're satisfied that your seam placements work best in the room you're working in. Sometimes, instead of making alterations and adjustments to your original layout, you might want to try several layouts, each beginning at a different point, to see which works best. This may seem like a delay in the process, but it is much easier to make changes to your layout with pencil and paper than after you've applied (or misapplied) sheets of wallcovering to the wall.

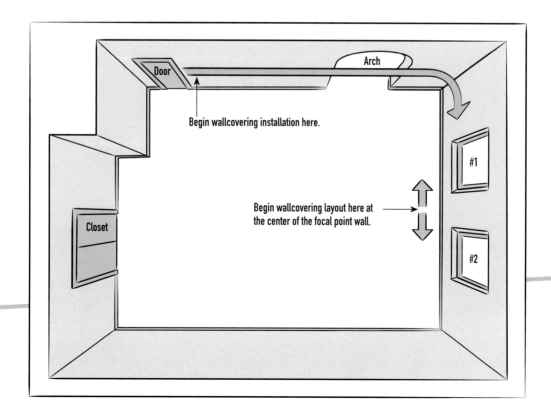

Door

Arch

Begin wallcovering installation here.

#1

Begin wallcovering layout here at the center of the focal point wall.

Closet

#2

Rules of Engagement

There are only two rules of engagement:
• Maximize the width of the strips of material applied to the wall (wide strips adhere better).

• Minimize the number and length of seams (fewer seams mean fewer chances for lifted paper edges and pattern misalignments).

Invoking these rules when working on your layout involves making a number of decisions and compromises. Here are some typical choices you may be faced with. Try to end up with more good choices than bad ones.

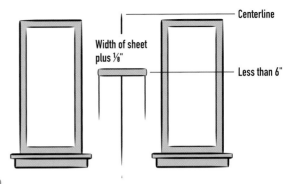

BAD

Centering a sheet of wallcovering between the windows results in two narrow strips of wallpaper adjoining the windows and two seams running the full height of the wall between the windows—the worst choice on two counts.

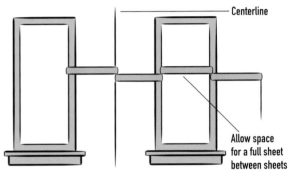

GOOD

This choice reduces the number of full-height seams between the windows to one and results in two wide sheets instead of one wide and two narrow—a better option.

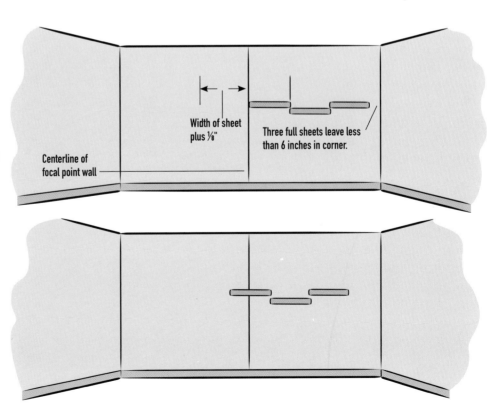

BAD

Aligning the edge of a sheet with the centerline of the focal point wall here leaves a narrow strip of wallcovering in the corner.

GOOD

Centering a sheet on the centerline of the focal point wall allows a wider strip in the corner.

My Mistake!

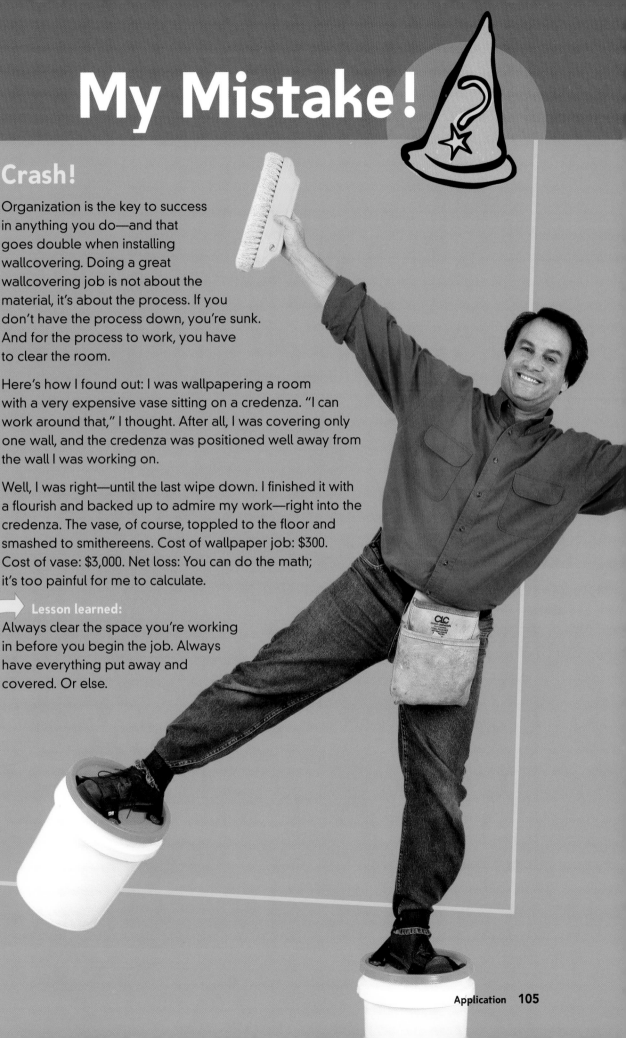

Crash!

Organization is the key to success in anything you do—and that goes double when installing wallcovering. Doing a great wallcovering job is not about the material, it's about the process. If you don't have the process down, you're sunk. And for the process to work, you have to clear the room.

Here's how I found out: I was wallpapering a room with a very expensive vase sitting on a credenza. "I can work around that," I thought. After all, I was covering only one wall, and the credenza was positioned well away from the wall I was working on.

Well, I was right—until the last wipe down. I finished it with a flourish and backed up to admire my work—right into the credenza. The vase, of course, toppled to the floor and smashed to smithereens. Cost of wallpaper job: $300. Cost of vase: $3,000. Net loss: You can do the math; it's too painful for me to calculate.

Lesson learned:
Always clear the space you're working in before you begin the job. Always have everything put away and covered. Or else.

Identifying the Focal Point Wall

The first principle says to begin the first trial layout at the center of the room's focal point wall. The focal point wall is the one your eye is naturally drawn to when you enter the room. That's generally one of these spots:

★ The portion of wall above a fireplace.

★ The largest section of exposed wall in a bathroom or kitchen.

★ The main section of wall in a kitchen eating area.

★ The first wall you see as you enter the room. The centerline runs down its middle (opposite page).

★ The wall with the room's main window or windows (often located opposite the door). If there is only one window, no matter what its size, it becomes the focal point, and the centerline runs down its center. If there is more than one window but they are on different walls, the larger window is the focal point. If there are two or more windows close together or side by side, the focal point centerline lies midway between them (opposite page). If you have corner windows or windows near the corner on two adjoining walls, they make a focal corner. Your layout starts at the vertical centerline of this wall. Once you identify the focal point of the room, use a No. 1 pencil to lightly mark the centerline at eye level. This becomes the starting point for planning a trial layout of sheet positions.

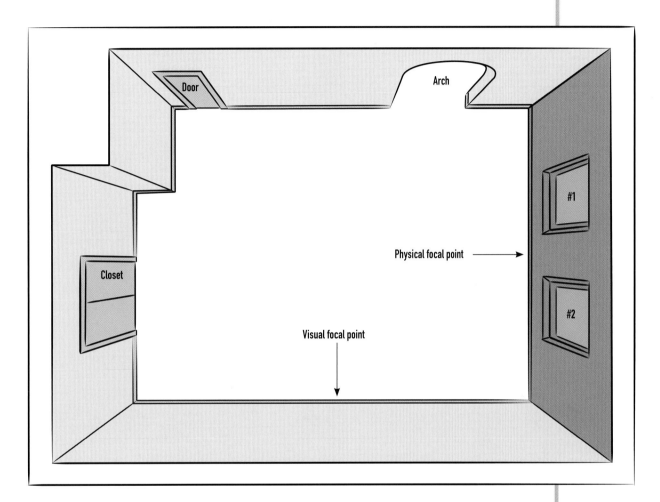

FOCAL POINTS IN A ROOM

Planning Vs. Doing

The starting point of your layout is not the point where you will start applying the wallcovering. That's an essential distinction: Planning the installation and doing the installation are two different processes, and they start at two different locations in the room. Deciding where to start applying wallcoverings will be done later. For now just realize that the two starting points are going to be different.

Creating a Trial Layout

Once you've determined your focal-point wall, you can create a trial layout that determines where each sheet of wallcovering will go. Here's how to do it:

1. Center the first sheet over the centerline of your focal point or align one edge with the centerline, whichever works best under the Rules of Engagement on page 104. Then measure and mark the seams lightly with a pencil for the rest of the room, adding ⅛ inch on average to allow for expansion when the paper is wet. Work from the corners of the focal-point wall to the dead corner.

2. Working from left to right, begin numbering the spaces between the marked seams in the order in which they will be hung. The first full-height strip will be sheet 1. This master sheet is the first you will hang, and it is the master pattern to which all other sheets will be matched.

3. Working from left to right, continue numbering the sheet positions around the room to the dead corner (2, 3, and so on) lightly in pencil. When you come to wide windows or other openings where you will split a sheet in two, label the upper section A and the bottom section B. Recessed windows or similar openings require duplicate sheets (step 6). Mark these sheets D. Number the sheets between the dead corner and the edge of the first sheet of wallpaper with negative numbers; those sheets will be hung from right to left instead of from left to right.

4. Once you have numbered each sheet location on the wall, measure the actual height of the wall in each slot in sequence, then add 4 inches.

Height Plus Four

"Height plus 4, height plus 4, you can't go wrong with height plus 4." I make those who attend my wallcovering seminars chant these words until they're seared into their brains. That's because one of the easiest mistakes to make when installing wallcoverings is to cut a sheet too short: Walls are rarely perfectly square, especially in older homes, and over the length of a room a slight angle to the ceiling or floor adds up. If you add 4 inches extra of selvage—2 inches at the top and 2 at the bottom—you'll have enough extra to cover for all but the most wacky, out-of-square rooms. So I repeat: The length measurement for each sheet that you enter on your layout chart is the height of the wall plus 4 inches, in every case.

5. Make a two-column chart on a piece of paper. Each horizontal line on the paper represents a sheet of wallcovering. In the left-hand column list each sheet number, starting with the lowest number (likely a negative number). In the right-hand column, write the length of each sheet.
This layout chart is the blueprint that will guide you throughout installation. It tells you how many sheets you need, what the length of each sheet is, in what order the sheets will be applied to the wall, and exactly where each sheet will be placed.

6. Recessed windows will not only require an A sheet above the window and a B sheet beneath the window, but two D sheets, one duplicating the sheet coming into the window and another duplicating the sheet coming out of the window, as shown on page 113.

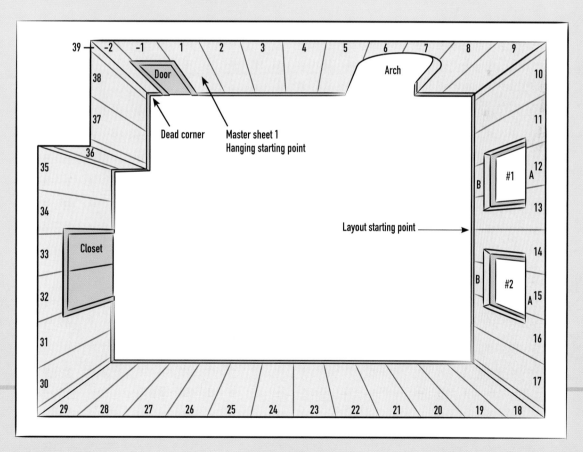

ROOM LAYOUT

Plotting the Layout

Plot your chosen layout onto the wall. First put light, penciled tick marks on the wall to mark where the seams fall. The spaces between the tick marks show where the sheets will be applied. We call these spaces *slots*.

1. Measure the room from the top of the baseboard molding to the bottom of the crown molding (if applicable) at each slot location. Add 4 inches to the actual measurement and note the resulting number of inches on your layout notepad next to the sheet number.

1

Use a Template!

Take a small, full-width piece of wallcovering to use as a template to help you visualize your layout. Unlike a stiff metal tape measure blade, the piece of wallcovering will wrap tightly around corners, giving you a more accurate sense of where the material's seams will actually fall.

Duplicate Sheets

You need to cut duplicate sheets in slots on either side of recessed windows and arches. Why? Because after you apply the sheets on either side of the window and the A and B sheets above and below the window, there will be two blank spots where there is no wallcovering at the top right and left of the window recess. You need two duplicate sheets to cover these patches: one that matches the pattern of the sheet on one side of the window, and one that matches the pattern of the sheet on the other side of the window. Both of these duplicate sheets are cut to the same length as the A sheet above the window. So for every recessed window you encounter, add a D sheet to your layout chart after the sheet for the slot before the window and a second D sheet to the layout chart after the sheet following the window (see page 113).

So your layout sheet should look like this:

11
11D
12A
12B
13
13D

2

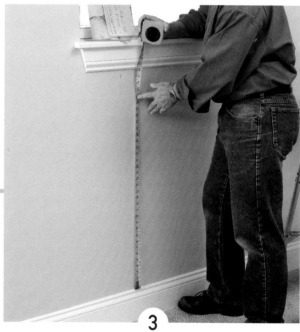

3

2. When you reach an interruption in the wall, such as a window, measure the amount of material required to cover the wall over the window plus the recess above the window. Add 4 inches to this amount and record the resulting number of inches on your notepad. Write A next to this sheet number.

3. Now measure the distance from the top of the baseboard molding to the bottom of the window molding. Add 4 inches to this amount and record the resulting number of inches on your notepad. Write B next to this sheet number. The number will be the same as the number of the sheet above the window because the sheet is within the same slot. Only the letter will be different.

My Mistake!

Keep your eye on the dye!

Numbers matter. Before opening a single package of wallcovering material, check the dye lot and the pattern numbers on the wallcovering itself. One digit off can make the difference between a great job and an unacceptable one.

When I was just an apprentice wallcovering installer, I worked for my grandfather. One of the first rooms I worked on required about 14 bolts of wallpaper. To save time (and you'll see the irony of that later) I read only the first four digits of the numbers on each bolt. They all matched, and I assumed the rest of the digits did too.

That was a bad assumption. When I finished the job and stood back to look at it, the room looked terrible. It turns out the numbers I had read were the pattern numbers, and yes, the pattern on all sheets was identical. But the last three digits—the ones I didn't read—were the dye lot. And it turns out I had bolts that came from four different dye lots. That meant every fourth sheet or so changed color slightly. And since this particular pattern was a dark, saturated color, you really noticed it. Your eye always goes to what's different, not what's the same. On this room's big, flat, open walls, the effect was dreadful.

Lesson learned:
I had to do the whole job over again—but I never again hung a single sheet of wallcovering without ensuring that the numbers matched—all of them.

Create a Blueprint for Success

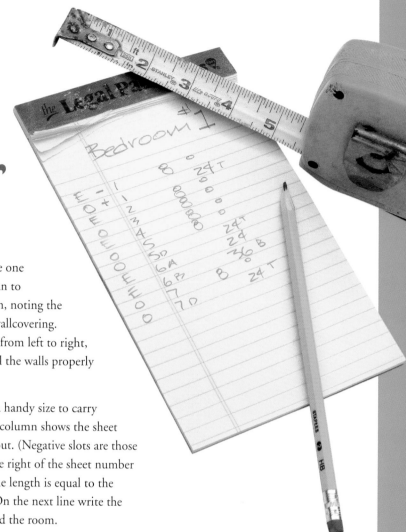

Once you've made several trial layouts and selected the one that works best in your room, you can commit the plan to paper. That means working your way around the room, noting the measurements of each slot that will receive a *drop* of wallcovering. Write down the sequential order of the slots, working from left to right, and the drop length required for each drop to cover all the walls properly on your written layout, as shown at right.

Create your written layout on a lined 5×7 notepad—a handy size to carry around. Each line represents one sheet. The left-hand column shows the sheet number, starting with the lowest number on your layout. (Negative slots are those to the left of the master sheet. There is no zero.) To the right of the sheet number and on the same line, write the length of the sheet. The length is equal to the height of the wall the sheet is to cover plus 4 inches. On the next line write the number and length of the next sheet, and so on around the room.

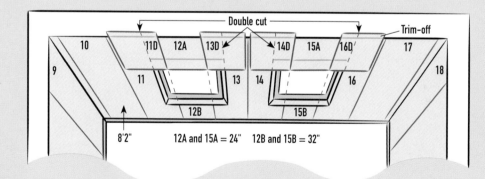

WINDOW LAYOUT

Remember that recessed windows will require an A sheet above the window and a B sheet beneath the window, and also two D sheets, one duplicating the sheet coming into the window and the other duplicating the sheet coming out of the window, as shown at left.

Precutting Wallcoverings

My grandfather, a lifelong wallcovering installer, used to say, "Wallpaper is a lot easier to deal with dry and flat than it is wet and vertical." He taught me to precut wallcoverings from bolts into sheets that were 4 inches longer than the wall they'd be applied to while they were still dry. That way, when it was time to apply them, they'd already be of manageable length and require only a slight trim once they'd been hung on the wall. Still it surprises me how many people—including many professional wallcovering contractors—wrestle with long sheets of sticky, slimy wallcovering. Don't be one of these people; precut and organize your material first. The job will go much faster, and a quality result will be much easier to achieve.

Teamwork

Here's where teamwork is especially important to the process: helping one another ensure that the material is cut properly. It takes two to handle and position large sheets of material, and two sets of eyes are important to double-check that the material is cut to the right length and numbered correctly.

STRAIGHT MATCH:

With a straight match, the master sheet is the sheet you hang first and the visual reference used to cut the rest of the sheets. Its length is the height of the wall plus 4 inches. Before cutting the master sheet, determine the key element in the wallcovering pattern.

To identify the key element, blur your focus a bit as you look at the pattern and identify the strongest element you see. It repeats throughout the sheet. (The large red rose is the key element in the pattern shown here.) Avoid cutting through the key element at the top of the wall. To ensure that the entire element appears at the top of the wall, leave at least 2 inches of pattern showing above the key element, plus another 2 inches for selvage.

WRONG WAY:
The cut bisects the key element.

RIGHT WAY:
The cut leaves 2 inches clearance above the key element.

1. Once you've cut the master sheet, leave it on the table. Then unroll the second sheet on top of the master sheet.

1

2

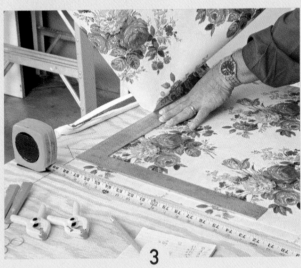

3

4

2. Check the left-hand edge of the master sheet against the right-hand edge of the material you've just unrolled. If the same element is in the same place on both sheets, your wallcovering material is a straight match.

3. Match the left edge of the material you've just unrolled to the left edge of the master sheet and cut the unrolled sheet to the length shown on your layout chart. The A sheets are measured from the top of the master sheet.

4. Cut all subsequent sheets in the same manner. Stack them directly on top of the second sheet you cut. Offset that stack slightly from the master sheet, leaving about 1 inch of master sheet showing to make sure you're matching the pattern with each cut you make. Number the sheets lightly in the upper left-hand corner using a No. 1 pencil. Check the numbers periodically to make sure you haven't skipped a sheet.

5. Measure up from the bottom of the sheet when cutting the sheets designated with a letter B. To avoid damaging the sheets underneath, cut the material by laying a carpenter's square across the paper at the cut point. Lift the paper along the edge of the square, tearing it neatly.

6. An alternate cutting method is to run a snap-blade knife along the carpenter's square. This method should be used only when cutting full sheets, when you are cutting directly on the tabletop, with no sheets underneath.

7. Remember to number each sheet after each cut. Once you have a neat stack of cut sheets on your table that correspond to the numbers of the sheets on your layout chart, you're ready to backroll the paper. Skip ahead to page 121.

DROP MATCH

Drop match patterns are cut in a different way than straight-across match patterns: There are two master sheets—odd and even. That's because the paper's design is spread over the width of two sheets.

1. Unroll the material on the table, determine what its key element is, and decide where to cut the paper, as with a straight-across match. In this case a border will be installed at the top of this wallcovering, so you must factor in the width of the border plus 2 inches of selvage to determine where to cut. That's so the border won't run right over the pattern's key element.

2. Check the pattern match on the right-hand side. The key element should drop by half the repeat on the right-hand side of the sheet. Double-check to ensure that it does, which tells you that you are, in fact, working with a drop match. With a drop match even-numbered slots will match one master sheet, and odd-numbered slots will match another.

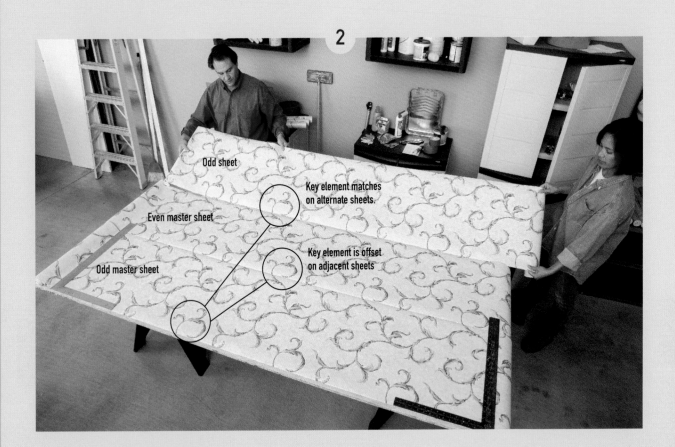

Odd sheet

Key element matches on alternate sheets.

Even master sheet

Key element is offset on adjacent sheets

Odd master sheet

3. When applying a frieze at the top of the wall, allow for the 2-inch selvage at the top of the sheet, here represented by the 2-inch-wide carpenter's square, and the width of the border above the key element before precutting the sheet. That ensures that the border won't run on top of the key element. Cut the first (odd) master sheet. Then match the drop pattern on the next sheet and cut it to length for the even master sheet.

4. To make sure you always match odd-numbered sheets to your odd-sheet master and even sheets to your even-sheet master, make a notation column directly on the table as I have in the photo. Odd sheets are designated O; evens are designated E; S stands for *stack*. Match all successive odds and evens to the two original master sheets, then put the successive sheets on the stack. Sheets 1, 3, and 5 have the key element in one position (under the pink knife), and sheets 2 and 4 have the key element in another position (under the orange knife). If you continually match odd sheets to the No. 1 master sheet and even sheets to the No. 2 master sheet, you cannot make a mistake and miscut. Cutting wallcovering by tearing it against a carpenter's square allows you to make a straight, square cut, and the square's weight keeps the paper from curling.

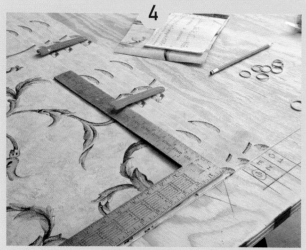

How a Drop Match Pattern Works
The snap-blade knives in this photo show where the key element is at either side of each sheet. Note that the key element drops by half the distance of the repeat from one side of each sheet to the other.

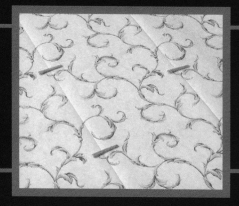

RANDOM MATCH

Because there is no repeating horizontal pattern, you can cut sheets continuously off the roll. Random match wallcovering is reverse-hung: The bottom of every other sheet is placed near the ceiling. That's because sometimes printing presses print one side of a sheet darker than the other. Reverse-hanging butts like sides against one another, preventing sharp changes in shade that would manifest as vertical bands if the sheets were hung with unlike sides butting. Keep track of the material's orientation by sketching a small arrow on the wall after the sheet number: an up arrow for sheet 1, a down arrow for sheet 2, and so on. Number the tops of each sheet when cutting, as for other types of patterns.

Mark sheet number in corner

Measure master sheet

Cut sheets to master

Cutting grass cloth

Natural materials such as grass cloth have no large, repeating pattern, so you can simply roll them out and cut the pieces to length. For that reason there's very little waste when applying these materials. That's a good thing because natural materials are usually fairly expensive.

Processing Wallcovering

After the wallcovering is cut, labeled, and laid on the worktable, it's ready for processing. Process the paper in two steps.

BACKROLLING

Roll each individual sheet from the bottom up so that the pattern is on the inside and the number on the back of the sheet is visible. Secure the roll with a No. 10 rubber band. Backrolling takes the twist out of the wallpaper sheet so that it will lie flat as it comes out of the water tray and exposes the prepasted side, allowing water to activate the paste. The number on the back of the sheet is easy to see, helping you to keep the sheets in the order in which you will apply them to the wall. The cylinders are easier to handle than sheets for the next steps.

SEQUENCING

The last piece of paper you cut will be the highest numbered drop. Usually it's the one that will be hung in the dead corner. Start the backrolling process with this sheet. Roll that sheet and secure it with a rubber band, then place it on the table beside you. It will form the first roll in a neat stack that you will build on the table. Continue to roll each succeeding sheet in descending numerical order, placing them side by side in order, until you have an array of rolls that is square. Continue rolling, stacking the next course of rolls at a 90-degree angle to the first. This keeps the stack stable. Continue in this manner until you have rolled all the sheets. Finally, backroll your borders and place them on top of the stack.

Activating and Booking Sheets

Booking allows you to work with a neat package of material rather than a long, unwieldy sheet. Before installing the wallpaper, you must activate prepasted wallpaper or apply adhesive to nonpasted paper. An important part of this operation is booking (folding) the wallpaper. Booking keeps the paste from drying out and prevents debris from contaminating the adhesive. It allows moisture to soak fully and evenly into the backing to promote better adhesion. Proper booking allows the wallcovering to expand evenly. It also makes the wallpaper easier to handle during installation. To speed up the job, one person can activate (or apply paste) and book the wallcovering while another installs it.

PREPASTED WALLCOVERING

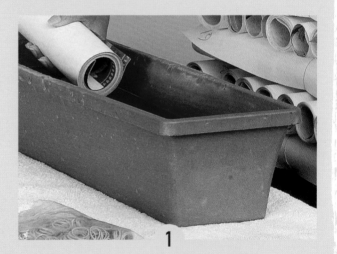

1. Fill a plastic garden planter box or water tray three-fourths full of water at 72 to 80 degrees. Warmer water will harm the adhesive and overexpand the paper; cooler water won't activate the adhesive. Remove the rubber band and loosen the first sheet so water can get between the layers. Soak the sheet in the water according to the manufacturer's instructions, timing it carefully. Oversoaking dissolves adhesive; undersoaking doesn't activate the adhesive.

1

It's in the Water

To better control the penetration of the water into the wallcovering adhesive, add some common household chemicals to your activating solution. For hard water add $\frac{1}{8}$ teaspoon water softener to 1 gallon water. For soft water add a capful of ammonia or 1 teaspoon of table salt to 1 gallon water. In the cases of all additives, don't exceed these amounts: More is not better. These additives have the effect of making the water wetter and better able to penetrate and activate the wallcovering adhesive.

2. Grab each corner of one end of the strip and slowly pull three-fourths of its length from the water tray, paste side up. Check the back for uniform wetness and splash any dry spots with water from the tray. Fold the top edge of the strip to the middle of the sheet, the pasted faces together. Align the edges, or seams, and smooth but do not crease the fold.

3. Slowly pull out the rest of the sheet. Check it for wetness and wet dry spots as necessary. Fold the bottom up and tuck it under the top edge so the ends overlap about 1 inch. This keeps the ends and middle of the sheet from drying out. Align and smooth as you did the top section.

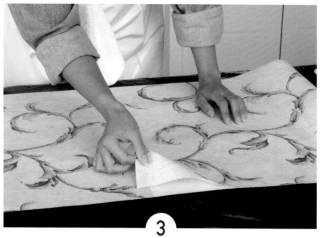

4. To book the wallpaper, fold the farthest fold to the fold nearest the water tray and repeat. The sheet is now booked. Activate and book five more strips to make a stack of six. Stack the booked sheets on a towel on the floor beside the worktable. Repeat for all sheets, working in sequence. Let activated sheets sit 5 to 15 minutes.

5. When you have booked a stack of about six sheets, flip the wet stack over and slide it into a plastic kitchen trash bag and close it with a twist tie to keep the air out and the moisture in. Now the sheets are in sequence and ready to apply to the wall. Sheets can remain in the bag until you're ready to apply that stack to the wall—a minimum of five minutes and a maximum of three hours. Leaving the wallcovering bagged any longer than three hours risks creasing the material. Write the sheet numbers on the outside of each bag and distribute the bags around the room near the walls to which the sheets will be applied.

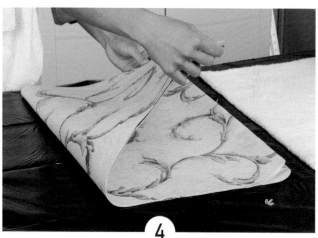

NONPASTED WALLCOVERING

Nonpasted wallcovering cannot be immersed in water because the materials are delicate and likely to stain. Some organic materials could disintegrate if immersed. Because of this, adhesive is applied in two steps to allow the paper to absorb the moisture necessary for good adhesion. Clear, ready-mix vinyl adhesive is the best choice of adhesive: It bonds well, is unlikely to stain, and is washable, so if it does get on something you can wipe it off.

There are two categories of nonpasted paper: vinyls and naturals. Vinyls have a vinyl surface and a paper backing. These are laid out, precut, backrolled, and sequenced in exactly the same way as prepasted wallcoverings. For this type of material, unroll and apply adhesive to the back of these materials one sheet at a time. Naturals, on the other hand, are precut, numbered, and rolled continuously from bottom to top. When you're ready to apply adhesive to naturals, simply unroll the entire stack with the natural side down and the backing side up on your worktable. Apply adhesive to the sheets one at a time, removing each sheet from the stack after you have applied paste to it.

Should I Paste Prepasted Wallcovering?

Absolutely not! Adhesives applied at the factory are carefully matched to the backing material. Adhesives have come a long way in the past few decades. Early prepasted wallcoverings didn't always adhere well, so some installers routinely applied a second layer of paste manually. That's no longer necessary and, in fact can cause problems: The adhesive you apply may not be compatible with the factory-applied adhesive or the material backing itself. Prepasted paper needs to be activated with 100 percent water. When you use an adhesive, the material ends up water-starved and can stick to itself during the booking process, destroying the paper. If you're applying wallcovering to a ceiling or high-moisture area, or if you're the belt-and-suspenders type who wants extra assurance that your wallcovering will stick, apply the paste to the wall—not the wallcovering—and allow it to dry. Then activate, book, and apply the prepasted wallcovering according to instructions. The dried adhesive on the wall will pull moisture from the adhesive on the wallcovering and result in an even stronger bond.

Ready your application table by assembling a regular paint roller cover, a roller tray, a bucket of clean water and a large sponge, and drying towels. Load the adhesive onto the roller as you would paint. Make a long stroke down the middle of the sheet and one down each seam of the material. We call this the *dump*. The next step, called the *set,* uses a W or an M pattern to spread the adhesive evenly over the entire back of the sheet, as shown below. The final step, called the *lay,* rolls the adhesive the full length of the sheet in parallel strokes to ensure an even coating over the length of the sheet. Cover the sheet in the three steps, then go through the three steps again. This ensures that there's enough moisture in the paper to prevent it from drying and sticking to itself during the booking process; it also ensures

that there's enough adhesive to bond the sheet securely to the wall. Double-pasting is a smart move: It takes only an extra couple minutes per sheet, but it is great insurance against poor adhesion. After pasting, book each sheet the same way you would prepasted wallcoverings after activation. Install booked natural sheets within two to three minutes to ensure that the adhesive doesn't begin to dry before the material is installed. Unlike vinyls, which absorb water only in their backing, naturals absorb moisture into the entire material and can dry out much faster than vinyls can. Book and bag two or three sheets of vinyl at a time. Keep a clean surface—if adhesive gets onto the table, clean it off with the sponge and water and dry it with a towel immediately so it won't transfer to the face of the material.

My Mistake!

Which end is up?

Whether you're installing a border or an entire wall, take time to study the pattern before you start installation.

I was installing a beautiful and highly elaborate floral wallcovering early in my career. I was most of the way through the job before I noticed I'd hung the pattern upside down.

It was an expensive mistake because, although I still had some paper left over, I couldn't get the same dye lot when I went back to the supplier, so I had to buy a whole room's worth of paper and throw out the unused bolts from my earlier purchase.

It's a mistake that's easier to make than you might think, especially with somewhat abstract florals. Here's how to tell which end is up: Highlights are always on top; shadows are always beneath. Remember that much and you'll never have to stand on your head to admire your latest wallcovering job!

Lesson learned:
The devil is in the details, and if you don't pay attention in the beginning of the job, he'll burn you in the end.

Activating and Booking Prepasted Borders

Book each strip in an accordion fold, paste to paste and pattern to pattern, and let it sit for 3 to 5 minutes. Roll the accordion fold, secure it with a rubber band, and place it in a resealable plastic bag for at least 15 minutes. This makes the border easier to handle when hanging and allows the adhesive to activate. Repeat for remaining lengths of border. Follow instructions for working with prepasted or nonpasted wallcoverings. Prepasted borders also require complete immersion in water.

If the border will go over existing wallpaper, unfold one of the border lengths and coat the back with a vinyl-to-vinyl adhesive, applying the adhesive as you hang the paper. Fold accordion style; repeat with remaining border pieces. Always wash the border and wall immediately because the vinyl-to-vinyl adhesive dries quickly and can ruin painted and papered surfaces. The following steps apply to prepasted borders:

1. After backrolling the borders and wrapping them with a rubber band, dip each individual border roll one at a time into lukewarm water in an activation tray for 10 to 30 seconds, following the manufacturer's recommendation. Slowly unroll about 6 feet of border, paste side up. This allows the water to saturate the adhesive and preshrink the border so that it will not curl at the edges.

2. Accordion-book the border by folding it inward in approximately 3-foot sections, paste side to paste side. This allows you to apply the border to the wall in manageable sections. Then loosely roll the entire accordion-booked border, and wrap it with a rubber band.

3. While your helper activates the next border, insert your accordion-folded, rolled border into a resealable bag. Once all the borders are activated, booked, rolled, and wrapped with a rubber band, seal the bag for at least 15 minutes. Don't remove the borders from the bag until you are ready to install them to ensure that the adhesive doesn't dry out.

The Three
Laws of Wallcovering

Here are the three inviolable precepts of applying wallcoverings. They're pretty simple, really. Follow them, and your job will go much more smoothly and, most importantly, you'll get professional results that'll look great when you're done—and for a long time to come.

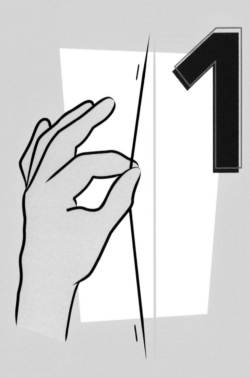

1 Every new wall gets a new plumb line.

Using a chalkline and a weight, mark a straight, perfectly vertical line that acts as the starting point on each wall. Aligning the wallcovering seam with the line ensures that the covering is hung straight up and down, no matter how out of square the room itself may be.

It also ensures that the alignment of each drop of wallcovering relates to the same standard, regardless of which wall it is applied to. That way there's no distortion of perspective between walls.

Use yellow chalk—blue chalk bleeds through the seams—and lightly brush away excess. Snap the line on the wall, where the right edge of the first sheet will be.

Cut inside corners; wrap outside corners.

Walls often are not square to each other, so folding a sheet around an inside corner can cause puckering and introduce crookedness. Outside corners are wrapped to avoid having an exposed cut edge that can lift or tear at the corner. Don't worry about pattern mismatches in inside corners; such a corner is rarely seen closely, so it's a perfect place to make up for out-of-square walls. As I often tell people in my wallcovering seminars, I love corners—they're great for burying any misalignment that may occur in a place no one is likely to notice.

Avoid overlaps.

Wallcoverings used to be printed with a blank edge that had to be trimmed by hand or installed with an overlap. Now wallcovering comes with precisely trimmed edges that are designed to be butted tightly against one another in order to create matching patterns and invisible seams.

There are a few more reasons not to create overlaps: Wallcoverings don't stick to wallcoverings well—they're designed to adhere to the wall itself, and overlapped seams will come loose. Overlaps also stretch and stress the material, which can shrink and ruin the seam match as it dries. Finally overlaps create highly visible ridges or bumps in the finish, which ruin the effect.

Getting the Hang of It

A sheet of wallcovering changes its name and becomes a drop when you hang it on a wall. A sheet is dry and horizontal; a drop is wet and vertical. Wallpaper is easier to install and adheres better if you handle it gently. Don't push, pull, shove, or press it in place to get a good seal; rough handling stretches the material and pushes the adhesive out of place, causing wavy seams that are more visible and corners that are more likely to pull away from the wall after they dry. Wallpaper dries in three to five days.

Every numbered drop of wallpaper goes on the wall in the same way. Place the ladder directly in front of the space where the first drop will go. Put the 4-inch broad knife, smoothing brush, and snap-off-tip knives in your apron or tool pouch pockets. Hang the first drop, then additional drops in sequence, following these steps:

1. Snap a plumb chalkline to mark the right edge of the first drop (top left photo). Climb the ladder and unfold the top portion of the booked drop. The weight of the folded bottom holds the drop straight while you work with the top half. Align the edge of the drop with the line. Let a 2-inch selvage overlap the ceiling. Position the key element 2 inches below the top of the wall.

2. Tap the drop into the ceiling line with the wallpapering brush and crease it into the corner with a broad knife so the 2-inch margin flaps onto the ceiling or molding. Then smooth the material on the wall with downward strokes of the brush.

3. Climb down and move the ladder out of the way. Open the bottom half of the drop and smooth it against the wall with the brush. Crease the wallpaper into the base molding so the 2-inch margin overlaps the baseboard. Trim the bottom, guiding the knife with the broad knife. As you trim slide the broad knife along the cut without lifting the cutting knife tip from the wallpaper.

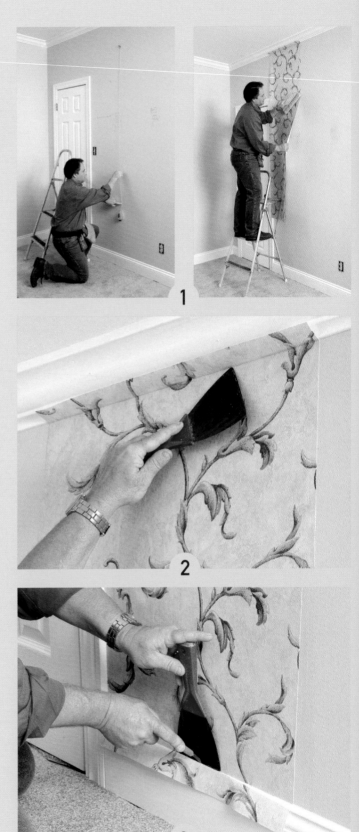

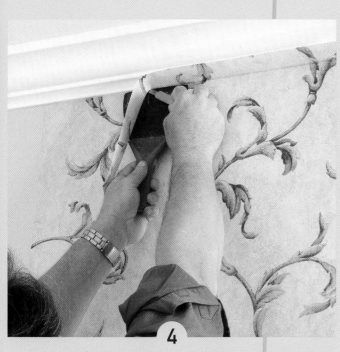

4. Using the broad knife as a guide, trim off the excess paper at the ceiling with a cutting knife. Start with a new snap-off knife tip for each cut.

5. Gently lift the edge and wipe away the chalkline. Smooth the edge back into place with the brush. Then brush the entire sheet one more time. If some bubbles won't work out, don't worry about them now. Most will disappear as the covering shrinks when drying. The goal is to eliminate air, not adhesive. Continue hanging drops around the room.

6. After installing two or three drops, wash the wall and molding with clear water and a sponge to remove adhesive residue. Wash from the top down. Dry the wall with a towel to reduce waterspotting. If you have a helper, the helper can wash while you continue installing drops.

Seams

Tight-fitting seams are the key to successful wallpapering; they are nearly invisible, giving continuity of pattern and rhythm. Don't overlap sheets—the seam won't adhere well, and the pattern will not align. There are two types of seams:

The butt seam is the most common wallcovering seam. The sheets butt snugly against one another, edge to edge. Don't put too much pressure on the seam as you smooth it down or you'll stretch the material out of square—and your seam will no longer be vertical. Even a tiny amount of stretch per sheet can be a problem, as the distortion compounds with each abutting sheet until it can create a very visible mismatch, the sense that your walls are leaning. Or the material will shrink as it dries, leaving gaps instead of tight seams. So brush seams gently and always vertically, never horizontally. Remember: When it comes to wallcovering, length is strength.

The double-cut seam is used for special situations, such as outside corners and borders. This seam starts with overlapping sheets. Using a carpenter's square or a straightedge as a guide, cut through both layers with the knife. Make the cut from the ceiling to the baseboard without cutting into the wall. Throw away the scrap from the sheet on top. Then carefully lift the edge of the top sheet and pull out the trimmed scrap from the sheet underneath. The two sheets will now butt together along the cut edges, and the pattern will match. Gently smooth the seam with your brush.

SETTING A SEAM

To set a seam brush it with a wallpaper-smoothing brush to eliminate air. Gently tap the seam with the bristle edge of the brush to tighten the bond. Then lightly pull a plastic float up and down across the seam instead of rolling it—a seam roller squeezes out the adhesive. The float levels the seam without squeezing out the adhesive. Always work vertically; going horizontally across the seam will pull the wallpaper out of alignment.

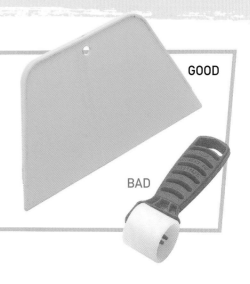

GOOD

BAD

My Mistake!

Doinngg!

OVERSTRESSING A TOOL CAN LEAD TO DISASTER.

I was using a snap-blade knife to trim wallpaper. It's the kind with a razor edge and a sharp point. You don't need to change blades when this knife is dull—you simply press sideways on the blade's tip and it snaps cleanly off, making a new sharp tip ready to cut. When you've used the entire length of the blade, you simply discard the blade holder. It's a great tool, but it deserves respect and it has its limitations.

Once I made the mistake of putting too much sideways pressure on the blade while I was cutting. Doinngg! The blade tip snapped off, flew up, and impaled itself in my cheek. I still have the scar. Had the tip landed an inch and a half from where it did, I might have lost sight in one eye.

Lesson learned:

Don't overstress your tools. And when you snap off an old blade, do it safely inside the pocket of a heavy leather work-apron pouch. The leather protects you from the sharp blade and the pouch keeps it from flying into the air—and retains all the used blades in one place so you can safely dispose of them when your job is done.

Turning Corners

Trim the wallpaper into inside corners, such as at the ceiling joint, at wall corners, when meeting moldings, and in similar places. Some of the pattern is lost in trimming, so the pattern rarely matches in inside corners.

CUTTING INSIDE CORNERS

When hanging the last sheet on a wall into a corner, split the paper into two separate pieces. This prevents the paper from buckling and wrinkling in the corner and keeps the pattern aligned vertically, though not always perfectly matched. Here's how to make the corner:

1. Install the left side of the wallpaper sheet on the wall coming into the corner. Let the right side overlap onto the other wall.

2. Crease the wallpaper into the corner. Using a 4-inch metal broad knife as a guide, slide your snap-blade knife down the inside of the corner to separate the two pieces. This method, called *scribing,* allows you to follow the slight imperfections of the corner as you cut, making them less noticeable to the eye.

3. Measure the width of the leftover piece. Subtract ¼ inch, then snap a plumb line on the new wall at this distance from the corner. Install the second sheet with its right edge against the plumb line. Overlap it onto the first sheet.

4. Double-cut the corner. The pattern won't match exactly in the corner, but your eye won't see the slight misalignment in an inside corner. What's much more important is to start with the first seam on the new wall absolutely plumb. By relieving a bit of misalignment in the corner, you prevent a larger mismatch on a butt seam in the middle of the wall. Also, over time houses settle, and walls may move independently of one another. If you don't cut the inside corner, the paper can pucker and wrinkle there.

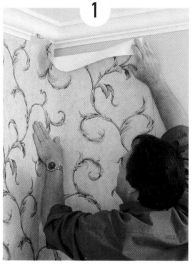

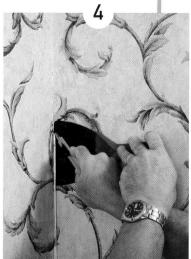

WRAPPING OUTSIDE CORNERS

Wrap outside corners to prevent the wallcovering from lifting off the wall when someone or something brushes up against it. To realign the pattern to fit the plane of the new wall, strike a new plumb line on the new wall; you will realign the pattern at the seam following the outside corner. That means the pattern will not match perfectly here. But in the case of an outside corner, aligning the pattern at the seam following the corner offers the best compromise between durability and aesthetics. The sheet numbers in the steps refer to the room illustration on page 109.

1. Measure the width of your wallcovering sheet. Subtract ¼ inch. Then snap a plumb line that distance from the last seam before the outside corner (the right edge of sheet 35). Apply sheet 36 to the wall, butting the right edge against the plumb line on the new wall.

2. Make a small vertical cut through the trim-off at the top and bottom of the sheet where it rounds the corner. This will allow you to smooth the sheet to the wall without wrinkles.

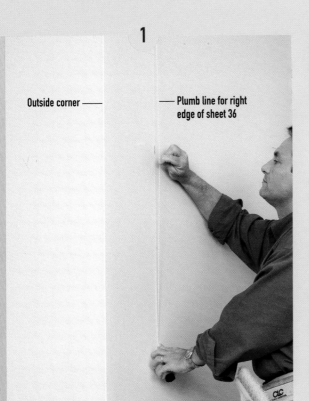

1

Outside corner ——

—— Plumb line for right edge of sheet 36

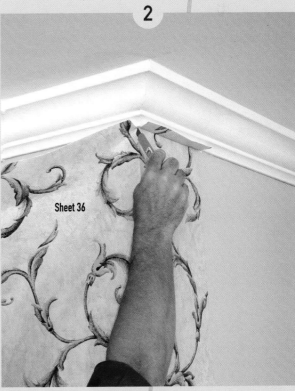

2

Sheet 36

3

4

3. Wrap sheet 36 around the corner, smoothing it onto the right-hand wall with gentle vertical strokes of your wallpaper brush. With the knife and long straightedge, make a double-cut seam where it overlaps sheet 35.

4. Remove the selvage from the top and bottom of the sheet by scribing and cutting to the ceiling or cove molding and baseboard using your 4-inch metal broad knife as a guide.

Ending at an outside corner

If you want to end the wallpaper at an outside corner, start by installing the wallpaper as if you were going to go around the corner but let the excess extend past the corner instead of smoothing it down. Hold the excess wallcovering taut with one hand and, holding your knife at a 45-degree angle and cutting from the face side, make a sliding cut down the corner. This leaves a clean edge that won't fray or peel. If you want to give an outside corner in a high-traffic area some additional protection, install corner protectors. They're available in both soft, colored vinyl or hard, clear polycarbonate. Both types have a peel-and-stick adhesive and are easy to apply. I prefer the polycarbonate type myself—they really take a beating and are almost invisible.

Cutting Around Trim

Secure the sheet at the top with your wallpaper brush. Working down from the top, make a series of small cuts at 45-degree angles wherever the sheet comes in contact with a piece of molding. These incisions, called *tension cuts* or *relief cuts*, allow the flat paper to fit around the protrusion and lie flat against the wall. Here's how the procedure works:

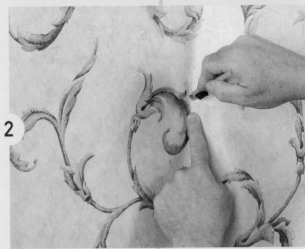

1. Hang the drop, leaving the bottom half booked. Press the wallcovering against the trim molding with your smoothing brush. The paper should now hang over the opening.

2. If there is a large amount of wallcovering over the opening, cut away most of the excess at the top half of the opening to get it out of your way. Then cut from the top corner of the molding with scissors to the edge of the wallpaper at a 45-degree angle. Make a very small cut—perhaps just a half-inch incision such as the one I'm pointing to in the photo. A relief cut should always be done with a fresh blade to ensure a clean and precise cut.

Before You Trim

Eliminate waves or bubbles in your sheet before you trim around moldings. Waves or bubbles will throw your trim cut off, creating either an overlap of the wallcovering onto the molding or, worse, a gap between the wallcovering and the molding. Wrinkles and bubbles are fairly common during this procedure, but fortunately, if you catch them and eliminate them before you trim, they're fairly easy to deal with: Simply lift the sheet up before you do the trimming and lay it down again, brushing it gently onto the wall. Once you're sure it's lying perfectly flat, make your trim cuts.

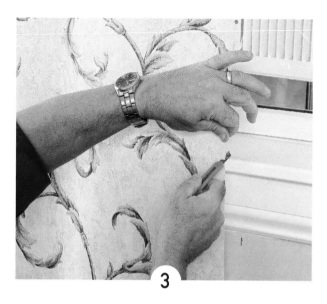

3. Hold the free edge of the sheet with one hand and make a sliding cut using the molding as a guide. Stop your cut when you reach the small incision you made in step 2.

4. Use your metal broad knife to protect the sheet and act as a trim guide when making a scribing cut around the moldings.

This is where the time and effort you spent caulking really pays off—you'll get nice, smooth, precise cuts that are almost effortless to achieve and look great. Working from the top down allows you to keep the paper parallel to the wall while progressively relieving the tension caused by the molding protrusions as you work your way down the wall.

Make It Snappy

Don't be a cheapskate when it comes to snap-blade knives. Before you make each new cut, snap a new blade every single time. Drywall, wood, and plaster dull the blades fast, and you need a razor-sharp edge to get a precise cut.

Knife tips are cheap. Wallcovering isn't. So cut, snap, cut, snap. When I'm done with a typical room, I've used hundreds of tips. I'll usually use one whole knife blade—that's 12 tips—for each sheet I hang. Since blades cost a buck a blade, or a little over 8 cents per tip, you won't go broke.

You can ruin $40 worth of wallcovering because you didn't spend 8 cents on a new blade tip. Most people buy a couple knives and use them until they're almost rusty—don't be one of them.

After the job, clean up the blade tips. I attach a magnet to a leather glove and go over the area and usually find a few small knife tips. You don't want to be pulling a blade out of the paw of your cat—or worse.

Recessed Windows and Doors

Wallcovering is two-dimensional but with recessed wall features, is taken into a three-dimensional space. That requires an additional technique: the duplicate method. This allows the pattern to match across the face of the wall and on the inside face of the window, and it allows the wrapping of all outside corners. The payoff is a beautifully maintained pattern and a durable, secure, long-lasting installation. That's particularly important around windows, where condensation and moisture can challenge wallcovering adhesion. Windows, doorways, wall niches, and other openings without moldings around them call for this treatment. Here's how to wallpaper a window; follow the same procedures for other openings. You will need a duplicate sheet for the sheet at each side of the window. The pattern of the duplicate sheet matches the pattern on the top of the full-length sheet beside the window exactly but is the length of the A sheet that falls in the next slot.

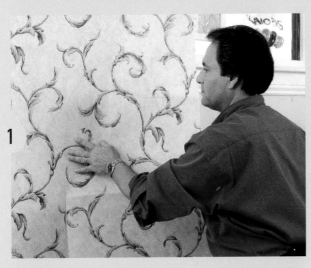

1. Hang the sheet coming into the window, number 11 in the room shown on page 109, allowing the sheet to overlap the window opening. Set the seam.

2. Make a sliding cut along the top and the bottom of the window opening with your snap-blade knife. This frees the portion of the sheet overlapping the window opening to wrap into the window casing. Smooth the paper into the casing, then trim off excess material.

3. Apply the 12A sheet on the wall above the window.

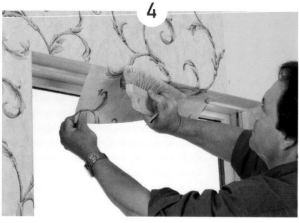

4. Wrap the 12A sheet into the window casing and smooth down.

5. Apply the 12B sheet on the wall beneath the window.

6. Apply the next full sheet, number 13, coming out of the window. Make sliding cuts at the top and bottom of the window opening and wrap the material into the window casing as you did in step 2.

7. With your aluminum carpenter's square, place the short leg abutting the ceiling and the long leg 1 inch inside the window casing. Cut through the sheet and remove the excess material. Repeat on the other side of the window.

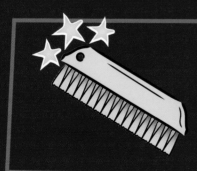

Fix Wrinkles, Not Bubbles

No matter how tempted you may be to pop a bubble in a drop, leave it alone. Adhesive generates bubbles through chemical action with water. As soon as the water content decreases through drying, the bubbles will go away. If there are wrinkles immediately lift the drop and adjust it until it hangs straight.

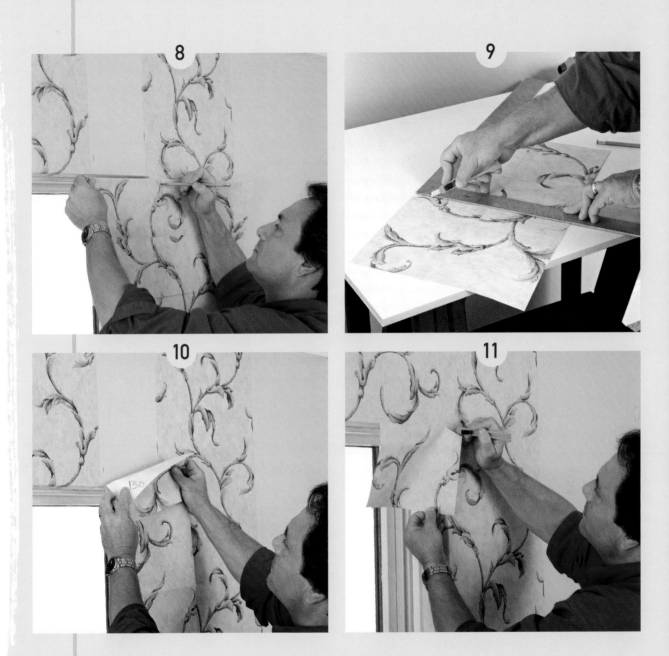

8. Make a mark on each of the two duplicate sheets 1 inch wider than the distance from the edge of the A sheet to the corner of the window on either side.

9. Use your knife and carpenter's square to make a vertical cut at the mark you've made. This is called *splitting a sheet*.

10. Position—*slot in*—the two duplicates by matching the pattern to the A sheet.

11. Locate the corner of the window and carefully make a horizontal cut from the corner to the outside edge of the wallcovering. This small cut will allow the paper to wrap inside the window casing.

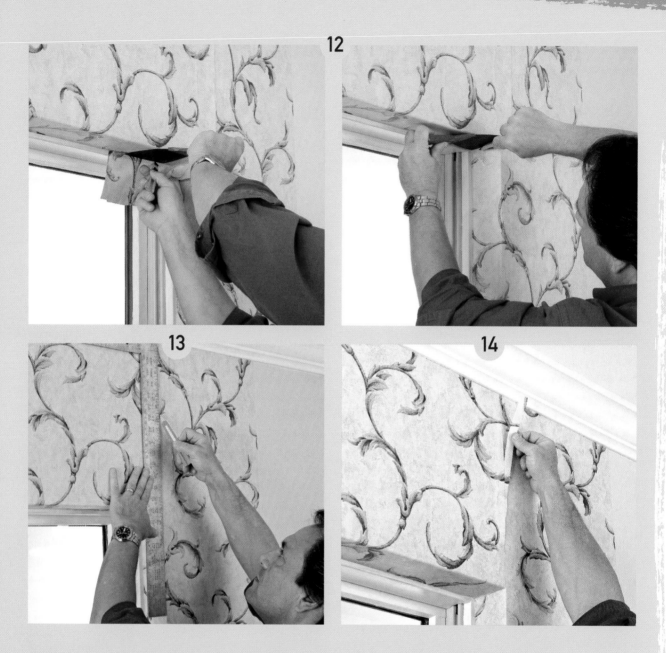

12. Trim off all excess inside the window. Notice that the pattern now matches, not only on the wall face but also inside the window casing. And this match wraps around the outside corner in accordance with the second law. However this has broken the third law: Avoid overlaps. But this is a special overlap—it's an exact pattern match.

13. Place your carpenter's square with the short leg square to the ceiling and the long leg precisely aligned with the edge of the window. With a fresh tip of your snap-blade knife, slice through both layers of overlapped wallcovering with one smooth cut, using the edge of the square as a guide.

14. Reach underneath the seam created by this cut and remove the excess both under and over the seam. The result is a perfect double-cut matching seam.

My Mistake!

Do-Over!

TAKE DOWN AS MUCH AS YOU CAN IN A ROOM.

Don't try to install wallpaper around easily removed features and fixtures, especially in bathrooms and kitchens. Remove the mirror, the towel bars, the toilet tank. Your results will be much better.

I was working around a towel bar that I should have taken down. I tried to cut the very thick wallcovering I was working with up against the towel bar stanchions, the part that attaches the bar to the wall. But the combination of the thick material, the bathroom's tight quarters, and the towel bar impeding both my vision and my working space resulted in me leaving a noticeable gap under each stanchion. What was worse, the paper was very dark; the wall underneath was blinding white. And the bright silver-colored fixture drew your eye right to the flaw. Needless to say the customer was not happy.

In an attempt to save the two minutes it would have cost me to remove the fixture before installation, I ended up doing the entire job over.

Lesson learned:
Yes you can cut corners when installing wallcoverings—but only inside corners. Don't cut corners on quality or you'll regret it.

Arches

Install wallpaper in an archway the same way as in recessed windows, but wrap the vertical sides only to the point where the curve begins. Cover the curve with a separate strip.

1. Let the drop hang over the opening. Hold the excess material taut with gentle pressure with one hand—be careful not to pull it out of plumb—and cut from the outer edge to the wall at a point just below the curve. Gentle tension will help you make a nice, clean cut. Gently brush the loose portion of the sheet—we call it the *wrap*—around the outside corner and smooth it onto the inside of the arch.

2. Trim away the excess material at the top and the outside edge of the arch.

3

5

6

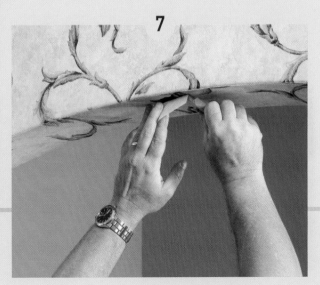

7

3. Continue applying paper across the wall above the arch.

4. Make a series of tension cuts at approximately 1-inch intervals along the remaining excess material, stopping the cuts ⅛ inch short of the edge. Wrap the tabs into the arch.

5. Measure from the apex (top) of the arch to the edge of the opening, then cut a new piece of wallpaper with the correct match for each side of the arch. The width of the paper should be equal to one-half the width of the arch plus 2 inches. Align the wallpaper and hang from the bottom to the top, trimming, slitting, and wrapping it as you did the first drop.

6. Trim off the excess material projecting outward from the arch with a sliding cut of your snap-blade knife.

7. Double-cut through the overlap of the material at the apex of the arch. Remove the overlaps. Smooth and clean. You have now wrapped all outside corners of the arch; you also have matched the pattern on the inside of the arch.

My Mistake!

Zap!

TURN OFF THE POWER TO EVERYTHING BEFORE YOU START WORKING IN A ROOM.
IF YOU DON'T THE RESULTS CAN BE FATAL.

Safety is my first concern, and I thought I had every precaution in place the day my wife and I started to remove three layers of wallpapering from the kitchen in a 1950s home. We'd run through our room preparation checklist, as always:

• Power off to lights and outlets? Check!

• Outlet and switchplates removed? Check!

• Outlets covered? Check!

• Rubber boots on for electrical insulation when working in wet areas, just to be doubly safe? Check!

So we started to work, wetting down the walls with wallpaper stripping solution. Pretty soon the walls were thoroughly wet and solution was running down and pooling on the floor. No problem—the floor was vinyl, and we were prepared to clean it up afterwards. We started peeling away long strips of paper. Everything was going according to plan.

But we'd failed to realize that in this house, the electric oven was hardwired to the fuse box on a separate circuit from the lights. Furthermore long use had baked the insulation off the wiring inside the oven, allowing current to leak onto the oven's stainless-steel cabinet. Even worse the oven ran on 220 volts— twice normal household voltage. Under dry conditions the wiring fault was undetectable. But water is an excellent conductor, and with everything soaking wet, conditions were ripe for a bad shock.

My wife barely brushed a wet arm against the oven cabinet, and BAM! The shock threw her back 10 feet and knocked her out cold. She had a concussion and was in shock. She recovered fairly quickly, but it wasn't a pleasant experience, to say the least. Had she made longer or more solid contact with the oven, she could easily have been killed.

Lesson learned:
Always have power off to every light and outlet—and to every hardwired, built-in appliance—before working in a room. That includes electric ovens, baseboard heaters, air-conditioning units—anything that runs on electricity.

Cutout Techniques

You will find electrical switches and outlets in any room you wallpaper. There may also be light fixtures, plumbing fixtures, or heating and ventilating grilles in the walls you are covering. Here are some tips on dealing with them.

SWITCHES AND OUTLETS

Turn off electricity to the room you're wallpapering at the circuit breaker box before starting the installation. Remove switch and outlet cover plates as part of the preparation for the project. Make sure water doesn't get into electrical boxes as you work. Water in a switch or outlet could pose hazards when you restore power.

As with door and window openings, install wallpaper right over the switch or outlet and smooth it in place all around.

In the opening make a vertical cut with the wallpaper knife parallel to the right side of the outlet and another on the left side. Pull the tab outward, then cut across the bottom to join the two slits. Cut away the tab at the top and trim the wallpaper to the edge of the opening on all sides. Lift and smooth the paper around the switch or outlet.

PERMANENT FIXTURES

Toilets, pedestal sinks, ceramic towel bars, and other items often can't be removed. When possible remove parts, such as the toilet tank, to make wallpapering behind it easier. Adjust your layout to put full-width sheets of wallcovering on one side or both sides of the fixture when possible. Use the star-cut method described on page 148 for light fixtures or to work around pipes. If you do have to apply wallcovering behind a toilet tank, use a yardstick held horizontally to pull the paper down flush with the wall.

REMOVABLE LIGHT FIXTURES AND THE STAR-CUT METHOD

If you removed the entire fixture and mounting canopy when you prepped the room, only the electrical box remains in place. (The electricity should be off.) Install the wallcovering over the fixture as you would a switch or outlet box. If the fixture or a protruding bracket remains, cut slits into the wall covering. For a large protrusion slit the covering from the nearest edge so it will slide around the obstacle. Work the covering into place around the box. Then lightly mark the perimeter of the box on the covering. Make a series of tension cuts that form a star from the center out to the perimeter of the box. This is called the star-cut method. Score the wallcovering into the opening with a 1-inch broad knife. Trim and smooth the remaining wallcovering around the box edge and seam the slit back together.

DEALING WITH THINGS YOU CAN'T REMOVE

It is best to remove everything from a room that you can before you start applying wallcovering. But there are some things you simply can't—or shouldn't—remove. Those include plumbing, embedded towel bar stanchions, wall-hung sinks and toilets—or, as shown here, a 220-volt electrical outlet and a gas supply pipe. Instead of removing these fixed and potentially dangerous items, work very cautiously around them. Always turn off the circuit to any electrical outlet in a room you're working in. If possible turn off the gas valve supplying any pipes you'll be installing around and bleed the pipe of the remaining gas so you don't risk a fire.

1. When you encounter a 220-volt switchplate, simply apply the sheet of wallcovering over it. Then cut through the wallcovering diagonally from point to point, forming an X. Using your 4-inch broad knife as a guide, score and trim off the resulting triangles of wallcovering. Smooth the surrounding area to the wall with your smoothing brush.

2. When you encounter an obstacle with a curved outline, such as this gas pipe and flange, use a star cut. Make a short slice beginning at the outside edge of the obstruction running toward the center of the obstruction every inch or so along the entire circumference of the object. Then trim off the resulting triangular tabs using your broad knife as a guide. This allows the wallcovering to conform to the outline of the obstruction. Smooth the surrounding area to the wall with your smoothing brush.

Carefully wash the obstacle and the surface of the surrounding wallcovering and rinse and dry it carefully to avoid stains caused by residual adhesive.

My Mistake!

Yikes!

KNOW WHEN TO LET NATURE TAKE ITS COURSE.
When things start to go wrong, sometimes the best thing you can do is to let them. An attempt at a heroic save can often do more harm than good.

I had just finished installing a strip of wallpaper in a kitchen with linoleum floors. More precisely I had almost finished installing it—I'd dropped my snap-blade trimming knife, so I couldn't trim the top. I had just descended the ladder to retrieve the knife when I noticed that the loose paper at the top of the strip was heavy enough to overcome the bonding strength of the wallpaper adhesive. The whole strip was starting to peel off the wall. Stupidly I leaped forward to try to prevent the strip from peeling, knocking over the ladder. If that weren't bad enough, I leaped again to try to catch the ladder. My feet slipped, and I fell full-force into the ladder. The ladder punched a hole in the wall, and the wallpaper strip peeled off anyway, covering me with now-ruined paper and slimy adhesive. It was a true Three Stooges moment. It hurt too.

Another time my trimming knife slipped out of my hand and started to fall. I reached out and caught it in midair, closing my hand on the razor-sharp blade. My elation at that save, as you might imagine, was quite short-lived.

Lesson learned:
Don't let your reflexes overcome your intelligence: If you drop a sharp knife, let it go. If something's falling on you, get out of the way. Reserve acrobatic saves for the tennis court, when the most you have to bruise is your ego.

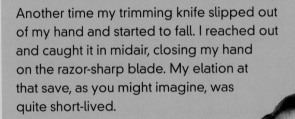

Ceilings

Whenever you wallpaper a ceiling, work along the shortest distance. For example in a 12×15-foot room, install the paper in 12-foot lengths.

1. Locate the center of the ceiling according to the focal point wall and snap a chalkline to mark it. Lightly brush away excess chalk.

2. Coat the ceiling with a thin coat of wallpaper adhesive and let it dry. This promotes better adhesion.

3. Wallpapering a ceiling always takes two people—one to hold the wallcovering while the other positions and smooths it. Start at the center of the ceiling. Otherwise the procedure is the same as for walls. Allow a 2-inch margin on each end of each strip.

4. If matching patterns hang the first ceiling sheet so that the pattern aligns with the pattern on the wall. They can match on only one wall, so make the match at the focal point wall. Trim and smooth. Repeat for remaining sheets.

Wallpapering Stairwells and Angled Walls

Stairwells are a common wallpaper challenge, and angled walls are wallpapered in much the same way.

Find the highest distance from the floor to the ceiling, usually two stories high. At this point lay out the area as you would for normal wallpapering. The ceiling is the horizontal line for the room, so for each strip of wallpaper, measure from the ceiling to the lowest point on the stairwell.

Working on a table that can accommodate the longest measurement, cut the first sheet. This is the master sheet and will be the first sheet to hang. Continue cutting strips to the correct length, matching the pattern and cutting waste. Install the paper; trim and smooth.

My Mistake!

Double your fun!

Here's something they don't tell you on the package: When you're installing wallcovering on a ceiling, always double-paste!

I once was working in a small bathroom where the client had specified using the same wallcovering on the ceiling as on the walls. The effect can be quite dramatic, especially in a small room.

This time the installation was dramatic. I'd done all the proper preparation, and meticulously too. It pays to be picky in bathrooms, as soap, makeup, and other residues can build up on the walls and wreak havoc with a wallcovering job if you don't get them all off with a good cleaning (see Chapter 3 for information on cleaning surfaces before applying wallcoverings). Also the high humidity present in most baths can deteriorate wallboard and plaster, so you need to inspect the surfaces carefully to make sure they're sound. I had done that.

On this job I was using a nonpasted wallcovering. "Good!" I thought. "That will let me use an extra-generous application of paste to make sure there's enough tack in the adhesive to keep the wallcovering where it's supposed to be—on the ceiling."

I slathered the paste on the back of the wallcovering, booked it properly, and started to install. I got only halfway across the ceiling with the first strip when the side I'd just installed started to peel. The only paper sticking to the ceiling was the part I was holding in my hands. Not a good sign.

Lesson learned: When applying wallcoverings overhead always put a layer of paste on the ceiling first and allow it to dry before applying the paste to the wallcovering and starting application. The dry adhesive will draw the moisture out of the wet adhesive and double the tack strength—making sure that what goes up doesn't come down.

Chapter 5

Finishing Touches

Even good wallcoverings correctly installed can do bad things, and often it's not their fault. Leaky pipes, steamy bathrooms, nicks and dings, pets, and children—life can take its toll on wallcoverings. But Wall Wizards keep a trick or two up their sleeves to correct some of that damage. This chapter shows some secrets that will help you care for and maintain your wallcovering investment. You'll also learn how to repair damage without having to redo an entire room.

The solutions to problems are based on the three laws of wallcoverings that you're already familiar with. And here's more good news: The basic skills and practices you've already used still apply, as do the tools and materials.

The first defense against a wallcovering crisis is to hang on to all the pattern numbers for materials you use. Staple the labels together, seal them into a plastic bag with the extra material, and store it all in a cool dry place to maintain the flexibility of the material and the adhesion value of the adhesive. When you finish your wallcovering installation, clean the tools well, let them dry thoroughly, and store them together so you can find them if you need to make a repair later.

Remember that repairing a wallcovering problem only fixes the damage; it doesn't cure the underlying problem. To prevent future damage ventilate that steamy bathroom, fix the leaky roof, or take the crayons away from the kids—at least when they're in the dining room.

Decorative Techniques

COVERING SWITCHPLATES AND OUTLET PLATES

By covering switchplates and outlet plates with perfectly matched wallcovering patches, you can almost make them disappear. And it's not that difficult. Here's how:

1. Attach the switchplate to the wall and scribe around its perimeter with a pencil. This outlines where the plate intersects the pattern on the wall.

2. Take a scrap of wallcovering that perfectly matches the area around the switchplate. Allow at least 6 inches of extra material on all sides of the switchplate. This allows for subtle pattern adjustments, and allows enough material so you can wrap it under the switchplate and adhere it securely. Dry-align the pattern to ensure that your patch contains the portion of the pattern that matches the surrounding wallcovering.

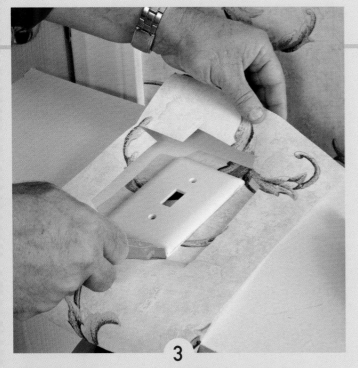

3

3. Following the pencil marks on the wall, find the four points where the corners of the switchplate intersect the pattern on the wall. Mark those on your patch. Make two cuts—one vertical, one horizontal—outward from each of the four marked points. The result is four tabs of excess wallcovering, one on each side of the switchplate. These tabs will secure the patch to the back of the switchplate.

4. Apply an even coat of spray contact adhesive to the back of the switchplate cover and to both sides of the switchplate. Let the adhesive dry for 2 to 3 minutes until it becomes tacky. Align the two top corners of the switchplate with the inside cut of the tabs on the scrap. Press the plate face firmly onto the back of the wallpaper. Lay the plate with the wallpaper attached to it facedown. Spray the back of the plate and the back of the tabs with spray adhesive. Let dry. Fold the tabs over onto the back of the plate.

5. In the switch slot make a vertical cut parallel to the right side. Repeat for the left side. Cut across the top and bottom of the opening and trim to the edge of the slot on all sides.

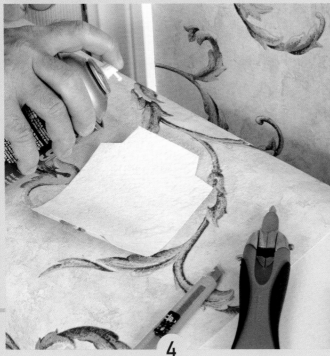

4

HEATING AND VENTILATING GRILLES

To prepare heating and ventilating grilles for covering, wash them with a solution of $\frac{1}{2}$ cup of TSP in 1 gallon of warm water. Cover the grille to match the wall by following the pattern-matching procedure for switchplates and outlet plates on pages 154–155. After adhering the wallpaper cut out the slots in the grille with a knife.

You also can paint electrical plates and heating, air-conditioning, and ventilating grilles with a color that matches or harmonizes with the wallpaper. Spray painting is the easiest and neatest way to do the job.

If you have covered an electrical outlet plate, you can paint the face of the outlet itself to match the wallpaper better.

BEFORE

AFTER

Instant Architecture

Borders along the ceiling, at chair rail height, or around doors and windows add interest to a room and can help separate colors and textures. A border creates a bold, graphic line in a room for your eye to follow. It really stands out. Here's some Wizard wisdom: Don't follow a wavy ceiling line. Use the drop-down method to hang the border in an absolutely straight line. Here's how: Measure the width of the border—say it's 6 inches. Measure down from the top of the ceiling $5\frac{7}{8}$ inches at each corner on each wall. Mark the spots with pushpins. Stretch a chalkline from pin to pin and snap a straight chalkline. Repeat for each wall. This transfers the ceiling line to the wall and creates the illusion of a level line. Hang the bottom edge of the border to that chalkline and trim off any selvage that wraps onto the ceiling.

PLANNING THE LAYOUT

Most borders come in 5-yard rolls. Plan your lengths accordingly, allowing for the ¼ inch of material lost when you cut inside corners and for matching the pattern at ends, if necessary. Buy more than you need. Check the pattern number and dye lot for each package. Friezes run on the wall just beneath the ceiling or crown molding. Dado borders are cut into wallcoverings to create special effects (see pages 160–161). Chair rail borders, also called *wainscot borders*, separate the upper surface of the wall, called the *body*, from the lower surface, called the *wainscot*. All borders generally start in the dead corner. Before you apply the border, check the material for flaws and back roll it, the same as for a wallcovering. Then snap horizontal guidelines to mark the border's location on the wall. Measure from the ceiling rather than the floor, as described above.

PREPARING THE WALL

If you install the border separately, prepare the border area with a primer/sealer, the same as for a wallcovering. Use the chalklines as guides. If the wall is textured, line the edges of the border area with blue painter's tape, then float the area with two coats of joint compound. This fills the surface texture on the wall to create a smooth surface for the border without changing the texture on the rest of the wall. Allow the mud to dry, prime it, then remove the tape. Apply the bottom edge of the border along the bottom edge of the smoothed surface.

FRIEZES (CEILING-LINE BORDERS)

Because the crown molding on this wall is fairly straight, I don't need to use the drop-down method discussed on page 157. Instead I align the border with the bottom edge of the crown molding.

Borders are easy to install with two people working together. Trim excess material along the edge of the ceiling. Smooth the border lengthwise, eliminating air pockets and helping the adhesive bond to the surface.

To match the pattern at the end, position a new length of border over the one already on the wall and align the pattern. Install the remaining paper to the inside corner and trim. Double-cut the wallpaper at the overlap; trim and remove excess material. Realign the pattern at the corner, trimming up to ¼ inch if needed, and continue around the room.

1. If two people are working, one person feeds the border to the other, who smooths it into place. Work from left to right, unfolding an accordion-fold at a time and aligning the paper with the bottom of the crown molding. Once you start to unfold the accordion, apply the border to the wall using a brush or sponge to smooth the border onto the wall. Brush or sponge along the length of the border. The goal is to eliminate any air trapped between the border and the wallcovering beneath. Be gentle. You shouldn't push so hard that you wrinkle the border or squeeze out the adhesive.

2. After installing the first roll of border, overlap the new border on top of the border previously installed, creating a precise overlap of the two patterns. Then cut through both layers of the overlapped material with one slightly wavy cut. A curved line makes the resulting butt joint harder to see when the job is finished. That keeps the pattern continuous.

3. Then, pull the waste material from the end of the first length of border from underneath the overlap. This is a double-cut seam; properly done it's nearly invisible.

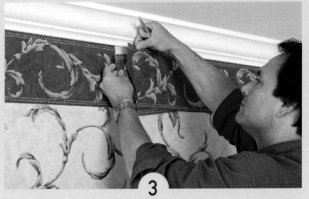

4. When you reach an inside corner, smooth the border into the corner, keeping the left side of the paper snug to the wall. In doing so create a small pucker—called a *back-lap*—on the right-hand wall. Make a vertical cut down the inside of the corner—called *scribing*—to separate the two planes of the border and keep it from wrinkling or lifting away from the wall as it goes around the corner.

5. Lift the left-hand side of the border and tuck it underneath the back-lap. That way if the wall moves, you won't see a split seam. If the back-lap is more than $\frac{1}{16}$ inch, cut into the corner to eliminate the back-lap so the border doesn't lift in the corner.

6. Set a 24-inch straightedge $\frac{1}{4}$ inch above the bottom of the border. Run a snap-blade knife along the straightedge, cutting through both the border and the layer of wallcovering beneath it.

7. Gently lift the border and slip the trimmed-off layer of wallcovering from beneath the border. Then smooth the border onto the wall. Now you have a single layer of wallcovering on the entire wall, and both the border and the wallcovering will have equal adhesion. If you install a border on top of wallcovering, it contracts and can pull off the top of the wallcovering sheet.

DADO BORDERS

The bottom edge of a chair rail border is usually 32 to 33 inches above the floor, the traditional chair rail height. However, you can center a wide border on a line 33 inches above the floor to maintain attractive proportions in the room. You can hang a dado border at any height; it can be especially effective if it aligns with architectural features, such as windowsills, or borders a chair rail molding.

Measure the width of the border. Then calculate the distance from the ceiling to the top of the border. Mark that distance at the corner of each wall and snap a chalkline between the marks. The top edge of the border will align with this mark. Repeat on all the walls in the room.

Dado Border Over Wallcovering

Snap a new guideline on the freshly installed wallcovering. Starting in the dead corner, set the border's bottom edge on this line. Using a painting shield as a guide, make a double-cut seam along the border's bottom edge. Lift the border, remove the excess base covering, and smooth the border back into place. Repeat to double-cut the top edge of the border.

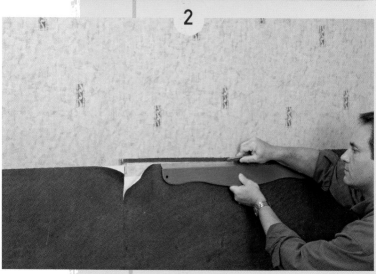

1 After applying the body wallcovering on the top surface of the wall, apply the wainscot wallcovering on the bottom surface of the wall. Overlap the two materials, then snap a chalkline along the middle of the overlap between the two materials.

2 Double-cut through both layers along the chalkline using a 24-inch straightedge and snap-blade knife. Remove overlapping material and smooth the resulting butt joint.

3 Using the drop-down method discussed on page 157, strike a horizontal chalkline. Install the top of the border flush with this line. Apply a vinyl-over-vinyl paste to the border and over the butt joint of the two materials. Make sure you rinse and dry excess adhesive thoroughly, as it can stain when dry.

Mitering Corners

You can create graphic effects using wallcoverings.
Here wallcovering with wide horizontal bands, free form
wainscoting, and a wide rainbow border combine in
a dynamic design. This could be a visual headboard for
a bed placed in a corner. The heart of this technique is the
mitered corner, which is fairly simple to achieve. Miter-cut
corners make the border pattern appear to be continuous
around the corner. Mitered corners are also useful in more
common situations, such as installing a border around
window or door moldings. In order to have enough border
for this technique, order 25 percent more material.
Here's how to make a mitered corner:

1. Cross the borders at the corner, leaving 2 inches beyond
   the intersection. Double-cut through the borders on
   the diagonal.

2. After cutting completely through both materials,
   remove the trim-off pieces from both above and
   beneath. This reveals a perfect miter-cut corner.

Creating Character

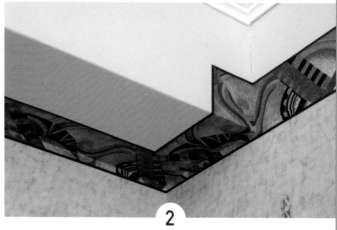

1. This frieze accents a soffit in the room by traveling along the lower edge and turning to travel along the face of the soffit. This creates a line that highlights an architectural element of the room.

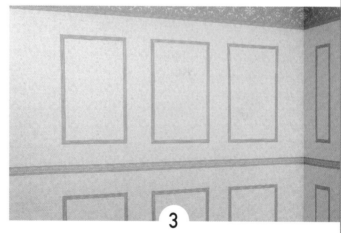

2. This border separates the top of the wallcovering from the painted soffit. This dado technique keeps the line continuous by running from the wall up onto the lower surface of the soffit.

3. This wall features a wainscot border at chair rail height. Cut-down sections of border are used as visual moldings to break up the wall space and add visual accents to the room, giving it a more sophisticated look.

Fine Touches

A companion material—generally a complementary wallcovering in the same colorway or collection—can accent a room's architectural features. Consider your room's architectural assets and how you might enhance them when choosing wallcoverings. Here I'm highlighting door panels with a marble-effect wallcovering.

Gee Whiz!

Wallcoverings traditionally have been printed on long sheets. They are usually applied to the wall in pieces that extend from ceiling to floor. ModulArt, a new option on the decorating scene, changes that. These 20½-inch squares of nonwoven polyester are sold in packages of six to cover about 17½ square feet. The prepasted squares are the easiest wallcoverings yet to apply because they're already cut into manageable-size squares. The squares also lend themselves to creative effects without a great deal of measuring, double-cutting, and waste. The opposite page shows how to apply ModulArt squares to create a dramatic harlequin effect. You could also apply them as stripes or larger single-color blocks. They are easy to cut with scissors, so you could even create curves or special shapes with them. And if you want to change the look after a while, you can peel the squares off the wall and reuse them.

1

Laser level

1. The wall must be smooth and properly prepared. Remove the squares from the packaging and backroll them. Activate in a water tray, following the manufacturer's instructions. Activate all of the squares you will use in one application session.

2. Continuing in the high-tech, cutting-edge vein, you can use a laser level to indicate a horizontal line on the wall in place of the traditional chalkline. It's a bit faster to use, and you don't have to worry about cleaning chalk dust off the wall. Place the first squares along the level line.

3. Filling in the next course, butt the edges together and gently brush the squares onto the wall. Brush firmly enough to eliminate any air bubbles but do not stretch or distort the material.

4. When trimming use a sharp blade, as the polyester is a little tougher than conventional wallcovering.

Repairing a Gouge

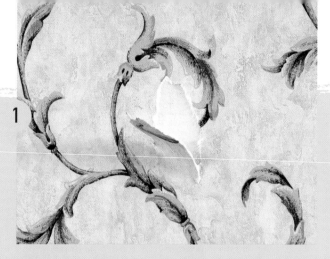

If the worst happens—you tear the paper when you're moving furniture, or some similar mishap occurs—do you have to strip the whole wall and install new wallcovering? If you rely on this Wizard trick, it's almost as easy to repair damage as it is to cause it in the first place. Here's how to make a repair that's almost invisible:

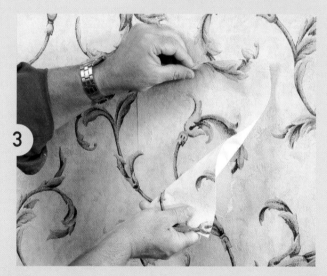

1. The size of the gouge or tear doesn't matter—small or large, the technique for repairing it is the same. This technique also works for wallcoverings that have been indelibly stained in a small area.

2. Find the area on a piece of leftover wallcovering that matches the pattern around the damaged area on the wall. Cut a patch from the leftover piece that extends at least 6 inches beyond the edge of the damaged area in all directions. Remove the torn flap.

3. Activate and book the patch you've just made. Carefully match the pattern on the wall to all edges of the patch. The pattern alignment must be perfect for this trick to work. If you misalign the pattern even slightly, your eye will go right to the imperfection. Take your time and get it right.

4. Lightly stroke the patch from the center outward in all directions with your float. Gently work the air out from beneath the patch but do not squeeze the adhesive out, stretch the material, or move the patch out of pattern alignment.

5. Using a snap-blade knife with a fresh tip, cut two intersecting crescent-shape cuts through the patch and the wallcovering beneath. This is called a *double-cut patch repair*. Cutting through the two identical layers with a single cut creates perfectly matched edges. Cut a football shape instead of a rectangle or triangle because your eye notices straight lines and multiple intersecting points more readily than curved lines. Keep the knife perpendicular to the wall.

6. You now have a duplicate piece of wallcovering that will replace the damaged piece. Remove the patch and book it again, folding paste side to paste side without creasing it. Put the patch in a resealable plastic bag. Then gently score or perforate the damaged piece inside the patch area. Mix a stripping solution of ½ cup fabric softener to 1 gallon water. Sponge this solution on the damaged area, cover the area with plastic wrap, and allow to sit for 20 to 30 minutes. The solution will break down the adhesive bond so you can lift off the damaged wallcovering. Do not damage the area beyond the patch or the cut edge, as that will ruin the effect. Remove remaining old adhesive from the area to be patched.

7. Remove the patch from the bag and smooth it into place with your float, carefully fitting it into the cutout area. Sponge the area down and let it dry.

Save the Remnants!

If you have a roll and some scraps left over, wrap them in plastic wrap, place in a plastic trash bag, mark it with the name of the room it goes in along with the pattern and dye lot numbers, and store it in a cool, dry place. That way you have material you can use for a patch such as the one shown here.

Repairing Seams

Seams usually lift because of exposure to moisture or lack of adhesive. Repairing a seam calls for applying new adhesive to replace the old and reexpanding the material so that the seams will butt neatly. Here's how to fix a seam:

1. Pull back the sheets to the point where they are secure.

2. Mix four parts of seam repair adhesive or vinyl-to-vinyl adhesive with one part water.

3. Using a small brush apply a thin, even coat of adhesive to the wall and backsides of the sheets. Leave the area open so that the water in the thinned-down adhesive will evaporate, causing the adhesive to get tacky. This usually takes about 3 to 5 minutes.

4

6

4. Apply a second thin coat to the wall and the lifted edges of the sheets. Again allow the adhesive to get tacky. Adhesives will not work when they're wet; they work best when they're almost dry.

5. Gently tap the seams with the edge of the bristles of a wallpaper smoothing brush.

6. Pull a float lightly over the seam to level the edges of the paper to ensure even and adequate pressure to allow the adhesive to bond properly.

7. Wash off any adhesive residue so it will not stain the paper. Rinse with clean water and dry with a clean towel to eliminate the possibility of water spots.

Seams Easy

For small seam lifts, add 2 ounces of adhesive to an ounce of water in a small container and stir. Gently lift the seam back to where it's secure. Wet the seam and wall with the solution using a small artist's brush. Wait three minutes or until the adhesive is tacky, then wet the surfaces again. When the second coat is tacky, gently set the seam with your float. Wash and dry.

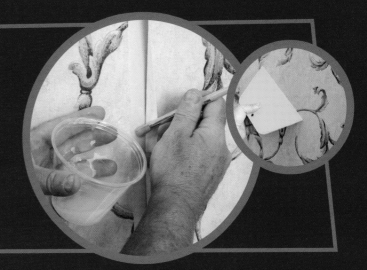

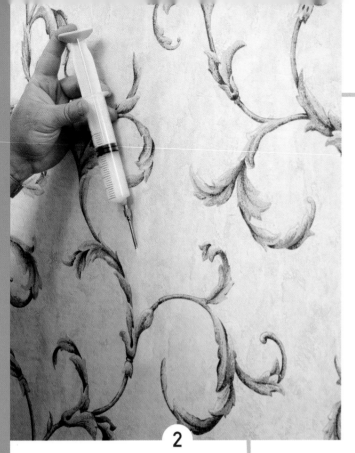

2

3

Eliminating Bubbles

Bubbles occur due to a chemical reaction—fermentation—that releases carbon dioxide as the adhesive dries. Bubbles are good because they tell you that the adhesive process is working. But the vinyl surface can trap gas against the wall like a tent. Most bubbles will eventually flatten out as the wallcovering dries, which can take anywhere from two to five days. So don't overwork the material and displace the adhesive trying to eliminate bubbles while the material is still wet. Wait for the adhesive to cure, then see if the bubbles remain. If some still do, here's how to fix them:

FOR SMALL BUBBLES

For bubbles between $\frac{1}{2}$ inch and 3 inches in size, try this technique:

1. Mix four parts of seam repair adhesive with one part water.

2. Poke a small hole with a needle in the bottom of the bubble. This hole will allow the air in the bubble to escape as I fill it with adhesive. Later it will allow excess adhesive to escape as well. Load a meat marinating syringe—available at kitchen and gourmet stores—with the thinned adhesive. With the syringe parallel to the wall, gently insert the needle through the wallcovering into the top of the bubble. Do not penetrate the wall. Slowly inject thinned paste into the bubble. Don't completely fill the bubble, just inject enough to wet the wall and wallcovering surrounding the bubble. Otherwise in fixing the bubble you may create a blister.

3. Carefully press the wallcovering back onto the wall with a float. Use three strokes: down to distribute the adhesive in the bubble, up to ensure complete distribution, and down again to force excess adhesive out the drain hole in the bottom of the bubble. Wash and dry the area thoroughly.

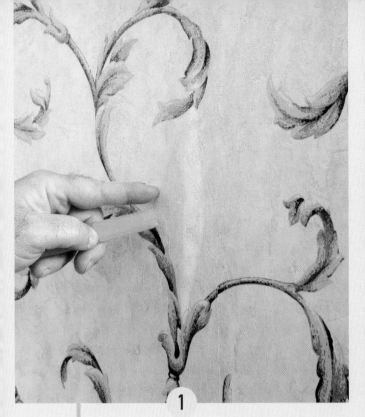

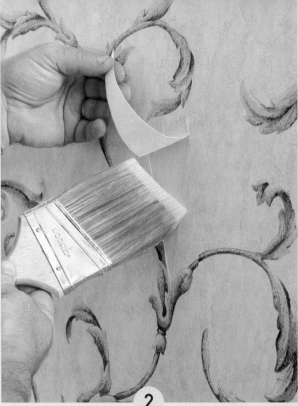

FOR LARGER BUBBLES

1. Cut three-fourths of the way around the edge of the bubble, leaving the wallcovering attached at the top.

2. Gently lift the resulting flap and apply a thin coat of the seam repair adhesive solution to both the wall and the back of the paper. Leave the flap wet and open. Let the adhesive become tacky, then reapply a second thin coat.

3. After the second coat of adhesive becomes tacky, smooth the flap down onto the wall with a float. Gently rinse and dry the area.

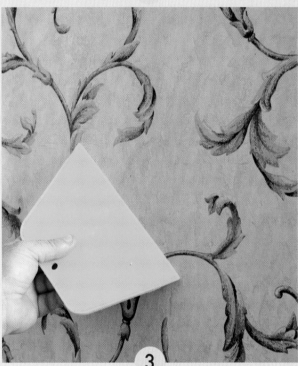

Cleaning Wallcoverings

Dust wallcoverings periodically to prevent dirt buildup. Most stains come out with a degreaser or spray-foam carpet and upholstery cleaner sold for home use. Test any cleaning product in an inconspicuous spot.

WASHABLE WALLCOVERINGS

Clean occasionally with a mild detergent solution (1 teaspoon of dishwashing detergent in a gallon of water) and cold water applied with a soft cloth or sponge. Treat stains before you wash the entire surface.

SCRUBBABLE WALLCOVERINGS

Scrub as often as necessary with a soft nylon brush and a mild detergent and warm water.

NONWASHABLE WALLCOVERINGS

Dry cleaning with rubber wallpaper erasers will remove many marks. For more stubborn spots blot the affected area with a sponge moistened with mild detergent and cold water. Don't scrub. Blot again with cold water and dry. If the stain remains ask your wallcovering dealer to recommend a spot remover. For overall griminess use a commercial wallpaper eraser. Ask your dealer about sprays to make new nonvinyl wallcovering stain- and dirt-resistant.

Wrinkles

The best way to eliminate wrinkles is to reposition the sheet during installation.

FOR WET WRINKLES

Smooth the wrinkle with a squeegee while heating with a hair dryer.

You can repair permanent wrinkles with the double-cut patch repair method.

FOR DRY WRINKLES

1. Preheat an iron at the polyester or permanent-press setting.

2. Hold a wet terry washcloth over the crease and press the hot iron over the spot.

3. Check the wrinkle every 15 seconds until it has softened but not pulled away from the wall.

4. Gently smooth with the plastic float. Repeat the process until the wrinkle disappears.

GAPPED SEAMS

To hide gapped seams rub the dry seam with a pastel artist's chalk that matches the wallpaper. Blot away the excess chalk with a terry cloth towel.

Index

Metric Conversions

U.S. UNITS TO METRIC EQUIVALENTS			METRIC EQUIVALENTS TO U.S. UNITS		
TO CONVERT FROM	MULTIPLY BY	TO GET	TO CONVERT FROM	MULTIPLY BY	TO GET
Inches	25.4	Millimeters	Millimeters	0.0394	Inches
Inches	2.54	Centimeters	Centimeters	0.3937	Inches
Feet	30.48	Centimeters	Centimeters	0.0328	Feet
Feet	0.3048	Meters	Meters	3.2808	Feet
Yards	0.9144	Meters	Meters	1.0936	Yards
Square inches	6.4516	Square centimeters	Square centimeters	0.1550	Square inches
Square feet	0.0929	Square meters	Square meters	10.764	Square feet
Square yards	0.8361	Square meters	Square meters	1.1960	Square yards
Acres	0.4047	Hectares	Hectares	2.4711	Acres
Cubic inches	16.387	Cubic centimeters	Cubic centimeters	0.0610	Cubic inches
Cubic feet	0.0283	Cubic meters	Cubic meters	35.315	Cubic feet
Cubic feet	28.316	Liters	Liters	0.0353	Cubic feet
Cubic yards	0.7646	Cubic meters	Cubic meters	1.308	Cubic yards
Cubic yards	764.55	Liters	Liters	0.0013	Cubic yards

To convert from degrees Fahrenheit (F) to degrees Celsius (C), first subtract 32, then multiply by $\frac{5}{9}$.

To convert from degrees Celsius to degrees Fahrenheit, multiply by $\frac{9}{5}$, then add 32.